T0167734

INNER YARDIE

ALSO BY PATRICIA CUMPER

Plays
The Fallen Angel and the Devil's Concubine
Horses of the Night
Buss Out (with Sistren)
Sweet Yam Kisses
One Bright Child
The Darkest Eye
Supple Silver
The Honourable All Purpose and the Dancing Princess (with Michael Reckord)
Flameheart
Chigger Foot Boys
The Ballad of John Simmonds

Adaptations
The Colour Purple
Their Eyes Were Waking God
Jane and Louisa Will Soon Come Home
Small Island
The Darker Face of Earth

PATRICIA CUMPER

INNER YARDIE: THREE PLAYS

THE RAPIST

BENNY'S SONG

THE KEY GAME

INTRODUCTION

KWAME DAWES

PEEPAL TREE

First published in Great Britain in 2014
Peepal Tree Press Ltd
17 King's Avenue
Leeds LS6 1QS
England

ISBN13: 9781845232320

Supported using public funding by
ARTS COUNCIL
ENGLAND

CONTENTS

To my son, Andrew, with thanks for his unstinting support over the years.

To my grandsons, Jaden and Cole, for always giving me a reason to smile.

In memory of Dennis Scott and Earl Warner whose bold, bright minds inspire me still.

INTRODUCTION

KWAME DAWES

Inner Yardie collects three very different plays by one of Jamaica's most gifted playwrights. They were written over a thirty year span – three critical decades in Jamaican history – and whilst the exact chronology of decades does not always match the shifting movements of culture, one can discern in these plays distinctive treatments of Jamaican society that engage with prevailing developments. Beyond this responsiveness to more immediate sociopolitical change, it is clear that Cumper remains committed to exploring the condition of the working class Jamaican in a longer view, in the context of the difficult and challenging experiences that emerge out of a history of slavery, colonialism and neo-colonial exploitation. I think that what we are observing in these plays is a movement from a certain kind of hopefulness to a deep questioning of the capacity of the society to change. While her characters always have agency and choice in their actions, there is a progressively greater emphasis on the forces beyond them that are profoundly destructive to their existence. Those forces, at least in two of the three plays, belong to what we can crudely call "the government". In *The Rapist*, whilst one can argue that the government plays a shadowy role in the narrative, it is distant enough from the action of the play to be almost ignored, but in *Benny's Song* and *The Key Game*, the governing forces are critical antagonists in the text.

I begin with the proposition that we are dealing with the same playwright whose ideology has been evolving over the years, even if it is an ideology predicated on constant and unwavering ideals concerning the dignity of the human being and the right of the oppressed and vulnerable to be protected from the predatory actions of those in authority. I assert this because of what should be obvious to readers: that each of these plays is stylistically quite different. The naturalism of *The Rapist* is followed by the broad spectacle and ritual-based staging of *Benny's Song*, which is in turn followed by the absurdist modernism of *The Key Game*. Of course, if nothing else, Cumper is a playwright who writes for her environment: the spaces in which her work is to be staged, the audiences who are expected to see the play and the era in which she is writing.

These plays were produced in three different eras. *The Rapist* was part of the beginnings of a popular commercial theatre scene in Jamaica in the 1970s, and stylistically the work reflects that context. *Benny's Song* was produced in circumstances that encouraged movement and spectacle in ways that the setting of *The Key Game*, performed on the London stage in 2002, simply did not permit.

In many complicated ways, *The Rapist* was a first on the popular Jamaican stage. Cumper's decision to tackle a difficult subject with what is essentially a comic vehicle reveals a great deal about the discourse concerning sexual violence in Jamaica. There is something unsettling about a play that humanizes a rapist, that locates the source of male violence within women, and that seems to diminish the horror of rape by elaborating on the motivations and by locating the effects of the violence offstage. Errol, we learn, is a rapist because he is constantly trying to rape his domineering mother. He is a rapist because he wants attention. He is a rapist because he wants to prove to his friends that he is neither gay nor uninterested in women. The reasons are less important than the fact that Cumper tries to find reasons, and the fact that the play ends with the location of Errol's deed as a manifestation of mental illness seems a softening of whatever feminist intent may have driven the play. But feminist insights are there aplenty, and an unusual plenty at a time and in a place when many of the speeches that Sharon makes would not have seemed in any way clichéd because they offer perspectives mostly new to Jamaican society, a discourse not yet familiar through later repetitions.

What Cumper achieves in *The Rapist*, though, goes beyond her exploration of sexual violence to present a nuanced study of 1970's Jamaica, with its growing crime, its political intrigue and corruption, its class and colour divisions, its gender and intergenerational politics. In contradistinction to a good deal of earlier Caribbean theatre, Cumper was not looking at the rural peasantry with its stock characters defined by stoicism, dignity, wisdom and local colour, but was part of a movement of playwrights of the reggae generation who were interested in the phenomenon of class relations within the urban lower and middle classes. The class spectrum of the play is relatively narrow, but complex. Errol's family is divided between a father who is content with a lower-class lifestyle, or what the middle-class brown family of the Williams would call "butu", and a mother who aspires to enter the lower-middle class. Indeed, Errol's mother's ambitions are intense and consuming, exemplified by her resistance to Errol taking a job as a mechanic – because they wear dirty clothes all day. Nor does she want her son lifting boxes in a grocery store. She describes herself as someone who lives by her wits, who will win because of her wits and calculation. She resents lighter-skinned women who, she believes, use their looks to get what they want. She is conniving, ruthless and selfish. Beyond that, she ends up being squarely positioned as the emasculator of her men, and the person singularly responsible for the sickness that leads her son to rape and brutalize so many women.

There is much that one could read as problematic in the construction of this character and in Errol's motivation, but what is undeniable is that Cumper creates characters who are convincing. Errol's mother is a type who seems familiar, whose class aspirations and the dismissal of the men in her life are believable, and whose motivations serve as a useful dramatic stimulus for the play. There is much to be said for this kind of approach in a play that was produced within a commercial context (and had a successful commercial run), that was traversing tricky ground at a time when, from the perspective of the present, some of the contemporary discourse about violence against women and the concept of rape is remarkably unsettling and uncomfortable. We are moving from the idea of "asking for it" as a pseudo-legal construct in the eighties and nineties to the clarity of "no means no" as a popular anti-rape slogan. In the play, Sharon is not ambivalent about what rape is, and she speaks boldly about it when she is challenged about liking Errol. When Errol's mother accuses her of enjoying what happened to her sexually, she is clear, asking how anyone can enjoy being beaten, brutalized and forced. Then Sharon lays out some of the core challenges to speaking out against rape, and in so doing, she articulates views that she knows are alien to Jamaican culture, but that she thinks are necessary and relevant. Here, Cumper uses Sharon to articulate what the emerging feminist movement in Jamaica was setting out to do. It had to first recognize the value of feminist ideas, even if they came from the imperialist west, and then find ways to apply them to the impulses and contexts of Jamaican women. Sharon speaks of hearing the words "character assassination" on television. It is an imported term, and by foregrounding this, Cumper appropriates the words into the discourse of her play:

> SHARON: Wh'appen, Dads. (Bitterly) You fraid fi scandal too… I know… I'm sorry… I know how it's goin' to be, don' worry; a girl at the office got rape las' month and she no settle down yet. Everytime she walk into the canteen, them seh: "Yes, that's de one. Is she get rape." And the jokes about how a woman can run faster with her skirt up than a man wid his pants down… Y'kno rape mus' be the only crime when the victim suffer more than the accused in court… Wat they call it… me see it on television all di time… character assassination… somet'ing like dat anyway… I don't know, father. It look like yu and dis old bitch a sing di same tune… Mi no kno…

That said, what one recognizes in early Cumper is a willingness to cast her characters in difficult situations and to complicate their ideas and feelings for dramatic effect. Sharon grows emotionally close to a rapist. This is the dilemma that Cumper introduces relatively late in the drama. But Cumper makes it even more complicated. She does not present this odd relationship as in any way a romantic thing. Indeed, the fact that Sharon comes to trust and feel cared for by Errol, who will then brutally rape her, means that she then has to contend with complex feelings of affection, fear, anger, and compassion in the midst of a charged situation.

Cumper's solution at the end of the play is ingenious. For her it is important to recognize Errol's victimhood. In the play's moral economy, the materialism and pride of Errol's mother, her aspirations to class promotion and to wealth, which she presses for at the cost of human compassion and care for others, almost constitutes a "sin" more abhorrent than the kind of transgression that Errol commits. For Cumper, Errol is a victim because emotional abuse and mental illness are not fanciful constructs or excuses. They are real, and while their consequences are often destructive for others, the play suggests that those who act under their influence should also be treated with care and compassion. Sharon's decision to testify against Errol is cast as an act of compassion – because he will have the opportunity for treatment – though given the horrific conditions of Jamaica prisons at the time, and even now, Cumper's solution here does seem rather idealistic, even naive. Indeed, one could even regard as absurd the presumption that Errol will get any kind of treatment for his propensity to rape in a Jamaican penal institution. Cumper, though, is not as interested in the logistics of the post-drama situation, as in providing an emotional motivation for Sharon's solution. Errol should be punished because, regardless of the fact that he is a victim of his own circumstances, he has raped and violated many women and his acts of violence should not go without consequence. More importantly, by testifying, Sharon will punish his mother, who is a genuine antagonist in the narrative. Establishing Sharon's action as merciful is, of course, confirmed by Errol's instructions to her through Munchie that she should testify. We are meant to conclude, I think, that, belatedly, the conversations with Sharon have worked on Errol's conscience.

> SHARON: (*Very angry*) Y'kno, me a go testify afta all… an yu kno why? Cause mi like yu son… Im hurt mi and I still hole a hatred in me heart for dat… but mi see now weh it mighta be di bes' t'ing all round if me jus' send him to prison one time and see wah 'appen. Mi don' see how he could be much worse off if he stayed with you… If im no go mad in jail, im

11

would a go mad wit yu aroun' im. So is might as well mi sen'
im dere, cause at least he cyan trouble nobody in dere, an' he
will be safe from yu and yu wickedness...

Benny's Song was a commissioned piece, and one that came with
some clear staging demands and opportunities. The play was to be
performed by the Edna Manley School of Drama – then called the
Jamaica School of Drama – and was to be staged in the very
imaginatively landscaped outer courtyards of the school. The
intention from the beginning was to create a play that made use
of the open spaces, the small hillocks, the trees, and the hedges,
along with the large sculptures that were littered throughout the
campus. At the same time, given the educational nature of the
institution, a large cast was desirable.

As Cumper makes clear in her introduction, the spirit and
nature of this production had a great deal to do with the experi-
mentation that directors like Dennis Scott, Eugene Williams and
Earl Warner had been creating in the theatre at this time, in their
effort to forge what could be called a Caribbean theatre aesthetic.
The School of Drama was the perfect location for such experi-
ments, and Cumper wrote her play in a context that offered
opportunities for a physical theatre of ritual and movement.

That context stood in distinct contrast to the kind of commercial "roots" theatre that was continuing to develop and become
increasingly successful in the 1980s. Such dramas, to be profit-
able, demanded smaller casts, accessible themes, simple, or even
simplistic staging, and a great deal of humour. However, it is
important to note that some playwrights committed to commercial success adapted to these changes while still trying to produce
works of "serious theatre". For instance, Trevor Rhone's plays,
Two Can Play and *The Game*, both had small casts, but sought to
capitalize on the taste for roots dramas without embracing the use
of stereotyped characters and unsophisticated staging. But in
general, plays became less interested in rehearsing the history of
colonialism and slavery, and more involved in observing and
sometimes celebrating the materialistic culture of 1980's Jamaica,
such as the popular phenomenon of the "Boops" syndrome that
valorized, to some extent, women who used wealthy men to
extract financial support from them.

By contrast, the School of Drama had remained faithful to a more ideological commitment to decolonisation and to a more experimental aesthetics. So, in *Benny's Song*, the typical constraints of commercial theatre were taken away from Cumper, allowing her to write a play with opportunities for spectacle, ritual movement and the choric use of voices. Further, given the commitment of the School of Drama to find innovative ways of refreshing a theatrical aesthetic that was rooted in the cultural practices of the society, the play opened itself to a staging that reflected the aesthetics and practices of the dancehall culture that was, at the time, overtaking and replacing the Rasta/Reggae culture of the 1970s. Cumper writes into the script several scenes in which the distinctive subculture of the reggae dancehall is enacted. The open staging allows her to locate scenes in streets and alleyways, replicating the peculiar street, yard and lane culture that is downtown Kingston. The power in the community is the don – the head of the garrison who controls its systems of justice, public morality and reward. Cumper finds innovative ways of drawing parallels between this subculture and that of Shakespeare's warring noble clans in the play *Romeo and Juliet*.

There is nothing especially innovative in the idea of adapting a Shakespearean play to one's immediate time and culture. The idea of locating *Romeo and Juliet* in an urban setting in which gangs are at war with one another had, of course, already had popular treatment, most famously in *West Side Story* (1957, 1961). So, in setting her version in 1980's Kingston, during the run-up to an election that has pitted two political parties against each other, Cumper is using a familiar formulae. The tragic love story that unfolds in such a context – one that brings lovers together from enemy camps – is inevitably going to carry the same message about the absurdity of tribal rivalry, and of the ability of romantic love (as a value if not an outcome) to transcend such barbarism. Cumper, however, is less interested in the love story – the notion that two young people can find sudden attraction and seek to defy the strictures of society and tradition – than in the forces that seek to separate the lovers. In other words, Cumper's approach grows out of her dismay at the ways in which Jamaican society in the 1970s and 1980s had become defined by the violent political battles that surrounded each election, and the ways in which such violence reflected the exploitation of the poor and how the exacerbation of their deprivations forced the poor to take sides in support of the politicians.

While Cumper could have put sweet-talking politicians on the stage, and could have made the lovers come from the families of the warring politicians – as the equivalent of the nobility who stand at the centre of Shakespeare's drama – she chose, instead, to people her stage with the poor, the foot soldiers of this war, and in so doing, she made a play about class, about race, about colour, and about the socio-economic forces that still affect Jamaican society. The larger forces that are manipulating the poor remain off stage, while on stage the ghetto characters are given agency and the potential for fuller and more complex renderings of their choices.

Of course, Cumper is writing within the complexities of Jamaican society. Her Romeo and Juliet, even while being work-ing-class individuals, are also socially aspiring people (at least Juliet is). She is a child of the ghetto whose fate, until she meets Romeo, was likely to be one in which she would be co-opted sexually by the don in the area, Para, who exercises his right to deflower all the virgins in the community, even as he serves as its protector, law enforcer and financier. But she is also going to school and her language is distinguished from that of her friends and the other people in the community by being closer to standard English (in the continuum that is Jamaican English). Here, Cumper employs a stock Jamaican class marker to establish her as "a nice and decent" girl, whose chance of escaping the fate of ghetto girls, like Arlene and Sweetie, is good enough to make the tragedy that ensues all the more poignant.

Of equal value is Cumper's analysis of the psychology of political patronage in Jamaica, which she tackles head on. Indeed, what is striking about this play is that Cumper explicitly names the two parties, the PNP and the JLP, as the forces at work. The stage is festooned with the flags, posters and clothing of these political parties – orange for the left-wing People's National Party and green for the right-wing Jamaica Labour Party. She also identifies what was happening to the dynamics of power in

Jamaica during that time – out of which grew the violence and criminality in Jamaica for the next three decades. In the 1980s, the power allocation that defined the relationship between politicians and the criminal sector began to change. Formerly, politicians held sway in controlling their henchmen, who were typically criminal types, during the off-election years, but who, nonetheless, were able to cement their power in their communities by being able to broker various kinds of benefits in housing, education, and jobs through their association with the politicians they supported as enforcers during the election season. However, with the rise of the drugs trade, beginning with ganja, moving on to cocaine, and the significant amount of wealth and weaponry that these local bosses were able to acquire, independently from the patronage of politicians, they soon became incredibly powerful and able to ignore efforts of politicians to control them in any way. This shift of power, which had full-blown public manifestation in the so-called Dudus-affair of 2011, when Christopher Coke, a latter day manifestation of Cumper's Para, managed to bring the country almost to a standstill during a violent stand-off with the government. In many ways, Coke and Para have a great deal in common, and in this respect Cumper's play offers us an important insight into the forces that would come to define the experience of Jamaicans in these "garrison" communities from the 1980s onwards – which is one of the reasons why the play still has so much currency. The speech that ends the play –given by the stock character of prophecy, the blind Missa J –somewhat heavy-handedly, but with bold clarity, offers the play's essential argument:

> For all yu sight, you no see it yet, old friend? For all yu sense, yu no understand nutting? Yu child dead before she even tun woman good and all yu can tink 'bout is death? And di whole a you, standing round di place like a flock a johncrow, wha' more you need to happen before you understand? Look, look and tell mi. Don't di two a dem blood red same way? Look again and tell me. Don't dem is young same way? If dem was born in a different time, in a different place, among people who no figet how to love and live, dese two young people would mek all a we proud. But look wha' happen now. Look wha' bring dem down

in di dirt now, fi dead like any mongrel dog a roadside. Dem did dare fi love dem one anodder, dem did dare fi try love when everybody a teach dem fi hate, try gentleness when dem no know nutting but violence and hatred. You know who responsible fi dem death? You know who? You! Di whole a you stand up deh and a look pon dem. You! Because you mek hatred rule you, you mek greed and vanity and spite run yu life. You poor and yu life hard and yu feel somebody fi blame fi dat. Somebody come yah and stand pon a platform and buy you curry goat and smile with you and tell you say yu problems come from dem over dere. And you tek you damn foolish selves and follow dem. Eat di goat and dance to di music and lose you self respect. Where dem is now? Dem is not here in dis graveyard. Dem is in dem house safe and sound […] And now dem going pinch piece offa di corner of wha' dem have to fling to you, mek you fight like puss and dog over it, mek you kill one anodder over it, mek yu disrespect yuself over it.

Whereas in *The Rapist*, Pat Cumper is willing to couch her ideas about gender and class within a largely comic framework, in *Benny's Song*, her intentions are more polemic, and more urgent. *Benny's Song* is a lamentation, I think, that expresses her troubled relationship with Jamaica and, perhaps, suggests the reasons for her decision to leave. In this speech by Missa J, Cumper expresses passionately both the despair and possibility that I think she felt about Jamaica:

Yu know when di killing a go stop? You know when you going to be free? When yu decide say no one, no politrickster, no gunman, no drug dealer, nobody going to tell you what to do. Cause you know. All of you know. Figet di vengeance. Figet di hatred. Look pon dem two poor young people. No mek dis happen for nutting. Memba everybody you know, everybody you care 'bout dat die through violence, and use dat memory to make you strong. If you do dat, tomorrow no matter which party have power, a we win. If you no do dat, yu blind more dan me. If dis no teach we say we haffi love di way dese two young people did love, den when we ever going to learn, lord? When we ever going to learn?

Missa J ends with a question, and it strikes me that the idealism of this appeal, the very idea that it runs up against – the all too real pressures facing people to fall in line behind the don men and the political powers – leaves us with the fear that the learning that Cumper's character calls for may never happen. Nonetheless, for Cumper, Missa J's vision offers a way forward, a way of hope that addresses what she sees as the core problem in Jamaican society – compliance to the exploitative and cynical power wielded by politicians.

At the end of *The Key Game*, in which Cumper shows she remains interested in the ways in which the actions of politicians and those with power damage the lives of the most vulnerable, a man perches on a ledge in a room, waiting for a bulldozer to destroy the room and, one presumes, to kill him. Whatever optimism we might have seen at the end of *Benny's Song* is replaced by this image of the collapsing walls of the stage. The man is Norman, the nurse, the sane one, the caretaker of three obviously mentally disturbed men, and yet it is he who, discouraged by the refusal of the government to provide resources to keep treating the mentally ill people in his care, has become, in a subtle but explicit way, the victim of great trauma. He, quite simply, goes mad.

The Key Game is, without question, a deftly written and sophisticatedly executed drama. Cumper credits the work of Beckett for her initial ideas about this play, but it also seems likely that she found some inspiration in the film *One Flew over the Cuckoo's Nest* (1975) in putting this play together. The fact that the play was completed after she moved to the UK, and first staged there by the Talawa Theatre Company, may explain its stylistic changes. At the level of language the difference is clear. Her characters are decidedly Jamaican, but they speak in a way that is wholly accessible to non-Jamaican speakers, with a vocabulary drawn mostly from the educated middle class. None of this is incongruous for the play. The characters *are* lower middle-class or middle-class Jamaicans. At least one of them has lived in the UK and returned to Jamaica. The main character, Norman, is a trained nurse, and an educated man who is trying valiantly to do the right thing, but who we see falling apart, slowly but inexorably, as the play unfolds.

Cumper's dialogue is sharply constructed. The strokes are subtle, deft and reflect a sophisticated awareness of the ways in which dialogue becomes the blueprint for action. She uses silences, subtle hiccups in speech and thought to create the verisimilitude of circumstance that she needs to convince us that we are in a real place, a credible place. After all, in strictly realistic terms, the premise of the play is not entirely plausible. There are only three patients on a whole ward – something wholly unlikely in Jamaica. Yet, the manner in which Norman seems to be controlling the entire staging of the play allows us to believe that perhaps the institution has long shut down, and that Norman, from his own pathological needs, has managed to create his own private asylum for these three men who, he sincerely believes, cannot survive outside without help. In other words, if we believe that Norman is lying about much of what is happening outside the room, we may be able to place credit in the circumstances that are placed before us.

However, Cumper does not give any explicit support for such a reading, so we must consider that we are expected to buy the story that the asylum is closing down, and that these three inmates are the last ones left, and they are left behind simply because of the ineptitude and heartlessness of the authorities.

Guilt, inner voices, the rituals of a compulsive disorder and the ticking time-bomb of the dwindling supply of medication, all serve as rich theatrical opportunities for Cumper to explore such volatile issues as sexual violence, homosexuality and mental illness in Jamaica. In the end, the prognosis for these characters is grim. Norman is going to allow himself to be killed by the demolition crew, and the three inmates are clearly not going to do very well on the outside because we know how hostile the outside is to them.

Cumper's writing here is rich and multi-layered. She complicates the emotional uncertainty of these men both through the coming closure and through their back-stories, which inevitably impinge on the present. But what Cumper never does is give obvious expositions of background and plot. Her characters reveal their histories through an oblique process of argument, deception and humour. She achieves this by allowing her characters to employ a highly figurative, but believable language, even as the dialogue slips into absurdist non-sequiturs, whose effect is a kind of controlled stream of consciousness. In the following passage, we see tenderness expressed by Shakespeare towards Gonzales who, it is clear, was responsible for the gruesome murder of his wife. Yet it is Gonzales who is granted some of the most elegant passages in the work. He speaks of love with a lyric intensity that necessarily draws attention to his pathology. Gonzales' poetic turns sit in contrast to the blunt pragmatism of Dappo and Shakespeare's earnest optimism, which we know is completely unreliable. The effect is nothing short of poetry:

> GONZALES: She was the first person that stayed with me. She loved me. She cared for me. She was my heart.
> DAPPO: Your heart is still beating in your chest, old man. You should listen to it sometimes.
> GONZALES: It tells me to go to the sea. I took her body and went out to beyond the breakers and gave her to the sea so she would be rocked forever. When I got back they stoned me. Chased me. Said I had lost my mind, disrespecting her body. But I hadn't. I had just lost my soul.
> SHAKESPEARE: You will find it again.
> GONZALES: I am too old to keep looking.
> (*He gets up and goes over to stand by the ward door.*)

At every hint of overblown language, Cumper undercuts it with a counter discourse: "She was my heart" is undercut by "Your heart is still beating in your chest, old man." This happens throughout a play in which the reliability or deceptiveness of language is an important theme. Through the character of Shakespeare she is allowed to introduce classical allusions which are put to good ironic use throughout the play.

Yet while the dialogue is where she locates much of her poetic power, Cumper's skill as a playwright is also revealed in the physical metaphors she creates on the stage through a series of repeated tropes and iconic gestures, such as the key game. The most striking, of course, is the one that ends the play:

> *Shakespeare departs. Norman tidies his desk and then the rest of the ward, then goes to the door. The bulldozers approach, rumbling and*

roaring. The flashing orange light gets brighter and brighter. Instead of going through the door, he locks himself inside the ward and climbs to where Gonzales usually perched. He takes the pebbles from his pocket and turns them over slowly in his hands. He is alone as the bulldozers close in and bring the walls of Ward 11 crashing down.

The ritual nature of this final scene is a striking moment of stage poetry. Norman has become the inmates in that moment, and he has arrived at the place of acute "un-madness" which is, as it happens, identical to "madness".

In this dynamic interplay between what is illusory and what is real, Cumper is returning to themes that we see in her two earlier plays, although in these she is exploring how perceptions can be warped in the context of a dramatic mode that is more founded on realism. In the earlier plays she asks such deeply political questions as what is rape, what is deviance, what is love, what is evil, and so on, and it is not impossible to deduce where she stands. In *The Key Game*, Cumper has fewer clear answers. Is Norman mad to simply allow himself to be crushed by the falling walls? Is his gesture morally noble or an expression of profound despair and surrender? That she does not answer these questions speaks to what seems to me a more complex moral positioning than exists in her earlier plays. In the speeches that end *Benny's Song*, we know that Cumper is unequivocal on the immorality of the political violence that leads to the deaths of Romeo and Juliet and many others, and in *The Rapist*, Sharon arrives at fairly clear moral answers: Errol is a human being worthy of compassion despite his brutal behaviour, and his mother is a despicable figure for her materialism and lack of a moral compass.

It is in this sense that we can see a progression in the complexity of treatment from one play to the next. Of course, this is something of an artificial reading since the context in which these plays were written and staged clearly has an important bearing on the kind of plays they are. *The Rapist* and *Benny's Song* were clearly written for the Jamaican stage and the Jamaican audience. Here, Cumper shows an appreciation for the interactive nature of the Jamaican theatre, where the audience often engages, literally, in dialogue with the characters on stage, and where the moments of dramatic discovery of truths need to be offered in timely ways throughout the play to sustain attention and, in many cases, to create humour. This is not, of course, to suggest that *The Key Game* would not have currency on the Jamaican stage, but it can be argued that the language, themes and theatrical style employed in it are more consistent with the modernist theatrical aesthetic that has a more secure place on the British stage. It is, I must hasten to add, not an alien style to Cumper, since it is one that she was well trained to explore during her time in the Caribbean working with playwrights and directors such as Earl Warner and Dennis Scott, who incorporated such modernist techniques into their own productions.

In the end, however, what we have here are three remarkably engaging and entertaining plays by a playwright of significant skill and authority. Pat Cumper's plays are nothing if not performable and revelatory in their exploration of Jamaican culture. As one of the first in what we expect to be an extensive play series, it constitutes an important addition to the currently slim body of published plays from the region.

CONVERSATIONS WITH MY INNER YARDIE

I write because I am angry. I say this with the clarity of hindsight. At the time of writing my first play, *The Rapist*, there is just an urgency to tell a story, a desire to explore ideas and themes, a pleasure in stretching creative muscles, a chance to be mischievous and say what I feel through a character of my own inventing. To write was to explore and understand my own duality, of belonging and not, being on the inside but seeing the world from the outsider's point of view. It was also a way of claiming a space that no-one else in my family had ever occupied, so freeing myself of the burdens of comparison and models of success and failure. It was access to a world that at the time I began writing was becoming more responsive to pure talent and was not a slave to class and opportunity.

If my anger was the grit in the oyster, the subsequent layers of nacre were laid down because of a range of other stimuli. I wrote *The Rapist* because I had been overheard by Ed Wallace, the producer of a revue of skits and songs, being critical of the show I had just seen. I was challenged to do better. I wrote a short skit that went into his next revue. I was asked to expand it into a full length play. I wrote it in less than six weeks and sent the script in without a name, then went on a family holiday. I came home to find that it had been called *The Rapist*. I had thought that Rosa was the central character, but the name made commercial sense and I hadn't myself suggested any other name for the play. It initially ran for nearly nine months and has been revived many times since; it was a surprising success for a play on such a dark subject. The lead in the initial production was played by the hugely popular stand-up comedian, Oliver Samuels, and audiences laughed until they cried. I would sit in the audience and listen to their responses at the moment when they realise that Rosa was actually being raped. The nervous titters, then the pin drop silence, taught me a lot. And yet, and yet, and yet – I did not think of myself as a playwright. I didn't dare describe myself as an artist. I made no serious investigation of what the role and responsibilities of a playwright might be. Critics and other theatre artists took my writing more seriously than I did myself. The critic Archie Lindo invited me onto the radio to talk about the play. He said that I showed promise and an understanding of character beyond my twenty-four years. I heard it all as criticism and not encouragement. Although I had been going to the theatre for as long as I can remember – at six years old I was that child who stood up and shouted "Look out! He's behind you!" into the silence of a polite audience at the splendidly Victorian Ward Theatre while watching the national pantomime – I knew nothing about actually writing plays beyond reading the works of Shakespeare and other British playwrights at school.

It would, however, be disingenuous to say that my confidence that I could write a play had no foundation. Ever since the Caribbean islands began declaring their independence from Britain in the early sixties, writers like Derek and Roddie Walcott, Dennis Scott, Trevor Rhone, Carmen Tipling, Barbara Gloudon had been writing Caribbean plays. I remember as a teenager sitting in the audience at the Creative Arts Centre on the Mona Campus of the University of the West Indies and being absolutely riveted by *Man Better Man* by Errol Hill, *Malcochon* by Derek Walcott and Dennis Scott's *Echo In The Bone*. Derek Walcott's *Dream On Monkey Mountain* was produced at the Ward Theatre, the work of Athol Fugard was produced at the Little Theatre, and every year a National Pantomime that used folk tales to explore topical issues and featured the best comic and musical theatre talent in Jamaica ran for months to ecstatic audiences. Theatre was often more a passionate hobby than a profession, but it was nevertheless driven by powerful intellectual and cultural forces. The forging of a cultural identity from our own experience and respecting our own synergies and histories was an urgent national and regional task. The politicians recognised it and cultural institutions were created and led by formidable personalities: The National Dance Theatre Company by Professor Rex Nettleford; The Little Theatre Movement – founded in 1941 but given a home building in 1961 – by Henry and Greta Fowler and Barbara Gloudon; the Jamaican Folk Singers by Olive Lewin. These were the leading lights. There were many others, organisations and individual artists, some that lasted, some that flowered and faded, but the intent was always much the same: to make a mark on this new page, to energetically eliminate the colonial and replace it with something more authentic, more true to our own history and experience. There is a case to be made that these institutions were about taking the rich and complex culture of rural Jamaica and the creative expressions of the urban poor and filtering it through a Eurocentric and predominantly middle-class lens in order to present a palatable cultural identity to those who attended these performances. It certainly felt itself separate from the – to my mind – more authentic music and roots theatre that was coming out of the ghettos of Kingston and drawing, at least initially, completely different audiences. But they met a real need for self-definition and contributed – and continue to contribute – to an island and even a region that punches above its weight and enjoys a strong if somewhat complex identity in the eyes of the world that some much larger islands and even nations do not have.

If the impulse to write *The Rapist* had been anger at my own family dynamic, the joy of it was exploring the language. Growing up with a Jamaican mother from an overachieving family of academics and teachers and an English father, an economist of wide and eclectic interests who had served in the second World War before settling in Jamaica, I lived in a standard English-speaking household. But the world around me spoke the dialect we called patois. The women I loved and admired – small farmers who worked with their hands and knew everything – spoke it. I would sneak my transistor radio into bed so I could listen to the radio serial *Dulcimina* by Elaine Perkins in secret, though in school I studied everything from Shakespeare and Chaucer to the Romantic poets. Music poured from the radio and we danced the ska, moonwalk, S90 skank, rock steady at our parties, alongside the soca, R & B and pop music sets that were played. All these things informed my writing. I had a concern that patois was seen as the language of comedy, of merry peasants and naive fools. I wanted to be one of those writers that used it to deal with weighty matters, philosophical questions, life crises, serious thought – like the performance poets Mutabaruka, Mikey Smith and Oku Onuora were doing. I would not say that I succeeded in *The Rapist*. But it began a journey.

For years after writing the play, this idea informed the hundreds of episodes of radio drama I wrote for Radio Jamaica and then Jamaica Broadcasting Corporation, daily fifteen minute episodes that won huge audiences, up to a quarter of all adult listeners by one survey. For the most part ignored by the theatre establishment, dance hall artists recorded songs about the characters from these soaps and I was delighted, when I drew up one afternoon beside a country truck laden with farm produce in a Kingston shopping plaza car park, to see that the driver had stopped and was listening riveted to an episode of the soap I had written and produced. I was fortunate to have wonderful actors to work with on these programmes, actors who understood what I was saying and enhanced it in a thousand subtle ways. When a leading character died, my script for the funeral episode was a list of hymns, the order of service and the eulogy. The cast took over and produced in a couple of takes one of the episodes of which I am most proud. The irony was that if I ever tried to read out loud the lines in patois I wrote for them, they would fall about laughing at my inability to pronounce the words correctly. Again that duality expressed itself. My ability to stand outside and write a range of characters meant that I was not on the inside of any particular group. I was a nice middle-class girl with a Cambridge education who was happy writing murderers and obeah women.

To have lived in Kingston during the 1980 and subsequent elections was to be angry – angry at the senseless loss of life, at the rampant political corruption and pork-barrel politicking, angry at having to live in fear amidst a fetid swirl of rumours of barbarisms and cynical cruelty. By the end, I could tell the difference between an UZI, a 9mm and an SLR just by the sound they made. *Booyaka*, shouted in celebration in the dance halls, copied the sound of a rifle shot and its echo. When I drove through many areas of downtown Kingston, my heart was in my mouth and I knew my progress was being watched, my presence vetted. Violence was a language in its own right and young men denied a place in society created their own hierarchies and systems of rough justice.

During that time, I had been fortunate enough to work with Dennis Scott, a wonderful barrel-chested playwright, poet, dancer and then head of the Jamaica School of Drama at the National Cultural Training Centre. It was he who, fixing me with his lighthouse gaze as he strode along a dusty sidewalk, asked me when I was going to give up trying to be funny and write about serious issues instead. I had to trot to keep up with him but it was his question that left me breathless. Did I dare be serious, take myself seriously?

Through him I met the Barbadian director, Earl Warner, a man who gave no quarter in critiquing my work. He pushed me to question the habits I had fallen into over the years as I generated reams of radio scripts, pushed me to refine my craft, and to tackle more important subjects. I had read everything I could find in book shops and on friend's bookshelves about writing for the stage and came to understand the basic three and five-act structures pretty well. I had attended a creative writing class led by the poet and critic Professor Mervyn Morris. He had said, and I took his words to heart, that each word must earn its place on the page by carrying forward character, plot or theme. I put this into practice in my playwriting, taking comfort in the discipline that way of thinking imposed, allowing myself very few flights of fancy. Consistently, the biggest note from Earl on the first draft of any play I submitted to him challenged that thinking. He urged me to let my characters loose to win over the audience, to let myself play with the themes and ideas I was exploring. He understood that much of the play was not yet on the page but had been left behind in my thoughts and imagination, and that for him and the audience to fully understand and engage with it, I had to be confident enough to let some of that thinking and imagining out for public scrutiny. His firm but fair criticism helped me build that confidence.

Bennie's Song was one of the many projects Earl and I worked on together and probably the most ambitious. He wanted a promenade piece that would use the students of the then Jamaica School of Drama – students drawn to the drama school from all over the island, often living on little and nothing, often at risk – who were passionate about making theatre. We needed a production that would address a subject close to their hearts, one that had roles for many actors, one that would stretch them intellectually and as performers. We decided on adapting *Romeo and Juliet*.

I thought Benvolio was the character in *Romeo and Juliet* whose journey might be changed without altering the central device of the play too much. I wondered what would happen to someone like Benvolio if he was pushed by the life he was living to the very edge? How would he cope? Could he remain the peacemaker? I created an arc for Bennie that began before the play starts with the death of his mother at the hands of Tibbie, Juliet's cousin, and ended with him laying down the gun he has taken up to kill Tibbie on his mother's grave. I wanted to weave the random brutality of party political violence into the heart of the play and this was the device I chose.

I was also concerned to create a moral voice in the play that did not reinforce the very hierarchical view of the nobility as intrinsically superior and the poor as the source of comedy and vulgarity espoused in Shakespeare's writing. The best I could do was to make the undertaker (who served the whole community whenever there was a death) and a blind musician (whose music offered some release in hard times) the carriers of the moral message of the piece.

Earl and I walked the grounds of the Cultural Training Centre to find out how best to set the play within them. We began by opening the back of the stage in the studio theatre so that actors could lead the audience across the stage to a playing area under the trees beyond. We found a site for burning tyres where the acrid smoke would not overwhelm the audience and, characterising the narrators as the carrion-seeking johncrows that hung in the skies over Kingston, we perched the actors playing them above the action wherever we could. Having led the audience around the centre by torchlight, we brought them back to the limestone amphitheatre at the entrance to the school of drama so that they could sit and fully take in the tragedy of young lives lost and hear the passionate plea that ends the play. These decisions informed the writing and rewritings of the play. My writing influenced the directorial decisions.

If *Benny's Song* lacks subtlety, it is because it is informed by the desire to change a society in which the value of life was so debased that tales of children sent to pluck gold teeth out of the head of a man dying of gunshot wounds in a Kingston gully might have been apocryphal but were no longer shocking. Yet it also sought to point up and celebrate the vibrancy and durability of Jamaicans living in poverty and dangerous times and places. Whether theatre that reaches only a limited and defined audience could have prompted any political or social change at all is another question. Maybe that is the artist's vanity: that what is created can in some way affect the society in which it is made. But is the play as a document of times and events, as a single howl into the moonless night, not worth something in itself? If it is a voice that contributes to the murmur, the swelling shout and then the demand for change, I wonder if that in the end is its best purpose.

To leave the country where your navel string is buried is difficult. To survive that rough transplantation into foreign soil, the immigrant creates a version of the home they have left behind in their head, heart and imagination. It is conjured up by those days when a moment of clear afternoon sunlight or the arch of a branch over the road reminds you of home, when an overheard voice or a snatch of music takes you back to childhood. The Jamaica I held, and continue to hold, in my being after moving to live in England exists nowhere else. I realise that. But it is still sufficiently rich in detail and anecdote that it informs many of the stories I wish to tell, it feeds the imagery I weave into the telling.

Before I left Jamaica, two deaths had affected me particularly. One of a close friend, one of a colleague. Both, it seemed to me, had on some level died because they were gay. That was one spark of anger. I had heard tales of men who slept with children to cure syphilis, of babies abused by family members, of fathers who

29

thought it fit to be their daughters' first sexual partner. I had myself, ever since I was a teenager, been forced to find my way around men who thought that inflicting crude jokes, groping and sexual harassment on the women around them were enjoyable aspects of their life. Another spark of anger. I had for years suffered from depression and worked very hard to cover it up because of the huge stigma associated with any kind of mental illness. My mother had spent years of her life drafting and redrafting legislation against stiff opposition not only to protect the rights of the mentally ill but also to prevent the proceeds of the sale of the prime property on which the national mental hospital stood going to any other cause but the treatment and care of those with mental illness. This too had made me angry.

My first exploration of the ideas in *The Key Game* happened in Jamaica. While rummaging around the bins of remaindered books in the Liguanea branch of Sangsters Book Store in Kingston I had bumped into Samuel Beckett and the absurdist playwrights and devoured them. Their unblinking gaze at the most painful, absurd and comic aspects of life was very like that of Caribbean writers and I read the plays, free of their European context, with excitement and found them inspiring.

My aunt, Fay Simpson, ran a ballet school and every couple of years would have a show at one of Kingston's leading theatres. She had asked me for any ideas I had for an original ballet she might choreograph and I had sent her an outline of *The Key Game*. It was, she said, too dark, too difficult. But the seed was planted in my head. When, several years after moving to live in the UK, I was asked by Talawa Theatre Company to send in an idea for a play I wanted to write, *The Key Game* came to mind. In it I could, through the characters, explore the effects of homophobia, the sexual and physical abuse of children and the attitudes of society to those with mental illness. I wanted to make the point that those who care for the mentally ill are themselves damaged when they are asked to enforce a system that they know will not adequately protect their charges. I also wanted to write a piece that made it clear that I could write male characters. Most of the protagonists of my previous work had been women. I suspected that made it easier to overlook my work, to categorise me as responding to a narrowly defined interest group, though I never felt that about my work myself.

There is a state you enter when you write in which time does not matter and the chatter of characters' voices is the only thing you hear, the world of the play is all you see. To be in that state is to be intensely alive. To be in that state is also to be oblivious of the world around you. Not all writing is like that. Sometimes it is a slog, an exercise in willpower where you summon all the craft you've learnt, all the determination your professional pride gives you to meet a deadline, to get the work done. *The Key Game* was written, finally, in that happy state. After years of writing small bits for radio, creating scripts from improvised or collective work, pushing away at doors that opened a crack and no further, I started from scratch in a society where my previous achievements meant nothing. I was being given a chance to write something of my own from start to finish, something that would be produced.

If *The Key Game* represented a play in which many aspects of my life experience and years of practice came together, it was also the first time I was talking to a British audience. I was no longer speaking with the voice of a majority. I was seen as a member of a minority, an immigrant from the Caribbean whose history, ethnicity and culture were seen as different, other – or that lovely word, exotic. I was more peripheral in this society than I had been in the Caribbean. The blessing was that being on the margins meant I could be detached in my observation of the mainstream; the curse was that whatever my observations were they were seen, by accident of gender and race, to be of little importance. Theatre, an art form that in Jamaica had been an arena for fundamental discussions of social and political issues, seemed to be more caught up in replaying its own archetypes to audiences with whom there was a tacit agreement about what these archetypes meant. Somewhat left of centre, more middle than working class, theatre comfortably reiterated its truths to its audiences.

But there is always, in the midst of that generality, something particular that can be seen as hopeful. One evening a group of young people came to see *The Key Game*. It was, I think, their first time at the theatre and they didn't seem to understand that the actors could see and hear everything they were whispering, texting and giggling about. They ordered pizza and went to collect it in the interval so arrived back late for the second half. Yet they stood up and applauded at the end. I saw tears on one girl's cheeks. If I had wanted to make them care about four men battling mental illness in a variety of forms, I had done that.

If I have created any space for myself in British theatre, it is as a facilitator, someone who creates space for the work of others, who makes the argument as to why to make Black work is not racist but instead a celebration of our diversity, who explains why this work of a minority – shaped by five hundred years of events in world history – should be seen at all, who puts her head above that parapet as a target at which the right and the liberal left aim potshots. For the most part, this has meant that I have put my own writing on the back burner, a source of deep frustration. Over the twenty years I have lived in England, I have come to understand that I am Black British, but it is an identity that is constituted differently from most of the other Black British theatre makers with whom I have worked. I am more guardian of the past and the future than participant in the present. Once again, the fundamental duality of my life and experience has asserted itself. And yet, and yet, and yet – I am a story teller.

To put pen to paper is to assert that you have something to say to which an audience should listen. That is the grit in the oyster, the little spark of anger that ignites the imagination. The language, the themes, the characters and situations, the sets, lights, costumes are all overlaid on that one impulse. They examine, test, reject, refine the story that is being told. The writing of a play is an act of persuasion, an invitation to the audience to enter a world, care about characters, to explore ideas, to feel some level of emotional catharsis. For much of my life, I have written plays. Because I could, because I wanted to, because there were stories I needed to tell. It is only lately that I have come to understand the power and profound importance of telling those stories in a world where there are too many unheard voices. An injustice unacknowledged is an injustice that will be repeated. My roots are planted back a yard and the Caribbean and the New World Black experience fed and watered me. Yet I am also the child of a scholarship lad from Burton on Trent who taught me to search for objectivity and see the bones of history beneath the skin of events. Now I have branched out into another society, I hold to my variegated roots and strive to grow under a different sky. And when something makes me angry, I will write. It is a matter of respect.

November 2012

THE RAPIST

The play was first produced in December 1978 by Ed Wallace Productions at Stage One Theatre in New Kingston, Jamaica. It was directed by Bari Johnson and Errol was played by the popular stand-up comedian Oliver Samuels, his first acting role. It ran for six months, at the time the third longest running play in Jamaica's theatre history. It was restaged in 1990 by Sun Promotions at New Kingston Theatre and was directed by Keith Noel with Carl Davis playing Errol. It was also produced at the Naparima Bowl in Trinidad by Acme Theatre Productions directed by Atiba Senghor.

CAST OF CHARACTERS

Sharon Williams – the central character. Twenty-two, fairly attractive, idealistic
Rosa Williams – her sister. Pretty, hard and grabby.
Mr. Williams
Mrs. Williams
Errol – the rapist
His mother
His father
Munchie – Errol's friend and a policeman.
Winston – Sharon's boyfriend

Sets

1. The verandah/front room of the Williams's house
2. The doorstep of the rapist's yard
3. Interior of Sharon's flat

TIME AND DAY CHANGES

Act 1
     Scene 1   Thursday evening
           2   Saturday midday
           3   The following Wednesday evening
           4   The same evening
Act 2
     Scene 1   That Friday night
           2   Saturday evening, the day after
           3   The following Thursday evening
           4   Friday midday

ACT 1. SCENE 1.

Thursday evening. Front room/verandah of the Williams' house. Middle-class, prim. Younger sister sitting filing her nails in her shortest shorts, hair in curlers. Radio beside her is very loud and she hums along. At intervals she takes up handmirror to inspect eyebrows, checks legs for shaving, etc. Her mother and father come as if from carport, talking to each other.

MRS. WILLIAMS: And there just wasn't any. No rice, no fat, no oil. I couldn't even find any soap powder. Y'kno, I remember the days when I could get anyt'ing I wanted at the supermarket.

MR. WILLIAMS: And she didn't even have the courtesy to apologise. She just threw the typing on the table and say she not staying this evening again. As if I ask her to stay every striking evening or something… no loyalty, the staff these days, just no loyalty, you give them a job and keep them off the streets and they can't even stay late one evening for you… it just doesn't pay to be reasonable anymore.

MRS. WILLIAMS: And even saltfish is so dear, when you can get it… I must just be too old or something, but I really can't take the traipsing around from one supermarket to the other just to buy some salad.

MR. WILLIAMS: Rosa turn down that damn t'ing nuh. Is bad enough I have to hear it all day on that system, but to have to come home to my yard… (*Rosa ignores him*). I really can't go on much longer like this. I don't know what can save this country from sliding downhill. It used to be that a man was respected if he work till he own a business. Now all them do is call you capitalist and cuss pure rass after you. And tell you bout union like union is any law. Do Rosa, mi seh to turn the radio off .

Rosa still ignores her.

MRS. WILLIAMS: Rosa… Your father said…

ROSA: Ah not deaf, Ma. Mi hear what him seh.

MRS. WILLIAMS: So jus' turn it off then nuh?

ROSA: You hear him say "please"? Even if I was going to shut it off, if he can't bother to show me no manners, mi can't bother hear him.

Rosa gets up and flounces off, with much backside wiggling. Sharon enters during this performance.

SHARON: Evening.

MRS. WILLIAMS: Rosa, come back here and apologise to your father.

ROSA: You sure he's my father? I don't see no resemblance.

MR. WILLIAMS: You facety bitch, apologise to your mother this instant.

SHARON: I said good evening…

MRS. WILLIAMS: Rosa, will you please…

ROSA: Lord, just get off mi back nuh. I bought the radio with my own money and if I want to play it I will, as loud as I FEEL like.

She exits slamming door.

SHARON: Ma, I said good evening…

MR. WILLIAMS: Rosa, get your arse back on this verandah before I…

ROSA: (*Putting her head round door*) BEFORE you what, father dear?

MRS. WILLIAMS: Rosa… Donnie… (*pleading to them both*).

SHARON: (*Shouting at the top of her voice*) I said good evening… (*Pushes past Rosa into house; all watch in amazement*).

ROSA: Well, well, well. What's eating her?

MRS. WILLIAMS: (*Heads after Sharon*) Oh dear, I better go see what the matter is…

ROSA: For a moment there I thought she was really your daughter, but it look like she have a little spirit after all.

She turns and goes inside.

MR. WILLIAMS: I just don't understand (*sighs*). In my day…

Noise of a car drawing up. Winston enters. He is very sharply dressed, a little on the vulgar side. He rounds the corner unaware that Mr. Williams is there, patting Afro and checking clothes.

WINSTON: Hi, Mr. Williams. What's happening with you?

MR. WILLIAMS: Better you ask me what isn't happening. This house is full of mad people, mad, mad, mad as rass. Why me, Lord? (*As if about to settle in to chat*). You know I can remember not so long ago when those two girls were little bit, little bit and quiet and obedient. I would come in from work and it would be homework, a little television and send dem to bed…

WINSTON: (*False*) Sure Mr. Williams, sure. Times changing fast these days eh? Sharon inside?

MR. WILLIAMS: Now, that was a really nice child. Not pretty or anything, but so quiet, polite. Never bother you with her chat and foolishness like that little bitch Rosa; she just did what she was told and that was that.

WINSTON: She here?

MR. WILLIAMS: Wah? Yeah man. Of course you should know by now. Where she have else to go but here? I will call her for you. Ah going in now. Women!… What did I do, Lord?

WINSTON: (*Humming to himself as he waits, boogying a little*) Yeah, old man, women. The more the merrier… (*sings*) is like a shadow… except me wouldn't want one so close behind me for so long… me like to move MAF-I-A (*sings soul*). "There's only one thing worse in this universe, that's a woman without a man…"

SHARON: (*Coming out onto the verandah*) Well, you feeling good today.

WINSTON: Honey, when you hot you hot…

SHARON: And you're hot nuh? (*Kisses teeth*). Lord, a tyad a it.

40

WINSTON: Tyad, girl? And your man is here to squeeze you and tease you and try his best to please you?

SHARON: Lord do, cut the phony accent nuh man. Mi no ha no patience with that today. Chu, me tired a it man.

WINSTON: (*Somewhat offended*) Tired? Of what? If you don't like my...

SHARON: Nah guy, is not you. (*She goes up to him and draws his arms round her*). Not you. Is this blasted house, man. I can't take it. All my father can do is tell us all how much better everything was once upon a time, and Mama – she stop listen to anything anybody saying except her self. As for Rosa. She's the hottest thing since Cleopatra, she and all her man friend dem. Me mussee either too old or too young to understand, but all mi know seh is me don't understand at all...

WINSTON: You were talking bout finding your own place...

SHARON: Bway, it look like that is what me haffi do. Lord, you remember the other evening on the verandah? Me nearly dead with shame. At my big big age, my mother is waiting up on me, and worse than that she come turn on light on me when we did deh pon the verandah...

WINSTON: And just when me did catch a nice little (*and he shapes after her breast*).

SHARON: Do! Mama probably watching all now too. Lord, Winston, when you brother going to country again? Me can' stan this hug up on verandah business. Me too old for that now.

WINSTON: You think is you? Don't feel no way, lady; I had to sit in the car and think about cold showers and such for a good little while before I could walk into the house. Why? You feel like a little...

SHARON: Chu guy, back off nuh. It isn't even dark yet. This is serious y'know. Mi haffi move out soon. You can live at home for just so long, and bway you haffi get out. Mi haffi find somewhere of my own, guy. I feel miserable these days, all the time, all the time so. I all argue with the people them at work for no reason, give the people wrong change… Chu.

WINSTON: So, what you fretting up youself about? You see anybody else getting upset? Jus' fine a place, rent it and then tell them. That's all.

SHARON: Yes, Winston… but Mama.

WINSTON: But Mama what? You think Rosa would worry bout Mama, Mama so? How you so soffi-soffi, girl? If you want get out, jus' get out, done, bam finish…

SHARON: It's not as easy as that, Winston… I mean… and anyway, I don't want to be like Rosa… she too tough for me sah…

WINSTON: I wouldn't call that tough…

SHARON: I know. If you never come here to check me, you would be into her baggy too, nuh?

WINSTON: Sharon: Is me and you…

SHARON: (*Kisses teeth*) I might be soffi-soffi, son, but I ain't blind. All the more reason to move out, nuh so?

WINSTON: Hey… Come here, woman… Stop bother up yourself bout them things nuh, and mek we do a little t'ing nuh. (*He moves in*). It don't look like the old lady deh bout, so come little closer nuh? How old you is, nuh nearly twenty-two, and fraid for you mother like puss still? Come mek me show you how we grown ups do it…

SHARON: Me no fraid, it's jus' that it don't feel right, not on the verandah with everybody inside. Fix up a little something for later nuh? But do, no more parking up y'hear… The last time when that man come and knock on the car window up on Skyline Drive me nearly dead with fright… Lord, you see how my life hard. I can't even…

WINSTON: Say it nuh… You embarrass, at your age… I don' believe it. I really don't. You should take a lesson or two from Rosa…

SHARON: (*Pulling away from him*) Rosa, Rosa. How you know so much about her. If she wasn't so blasted selfish, life in this house would be a little easier...

WINSTON: But since you are moving out of this house ...

SHARON: Yeah, I suppose... (*Goes back into his arms*). Chu. Andy wouldn't lend you his place tonight? I feel like holding on to somebody tonight...

WINSTON: Somebody... somebody huh. I see...

SHARON: Do, Winston. Don't bother fuss up yourself. Jus' check the guy nuh. Alright? And call me when you find out, alright. I going to look through the *Gleaner* for a place. Might as well start now, right?

WINSTON: Alright, daughter. More time. The man will call later and tell you wh'appen, alright.

SHARON: Alright... (*He goes*). Oh, and Winston... Chu him gone, and I wanted to ask him something too. Well it'll just have to wait till later. (*She goes over to sit on edge of verandah. Thoughtful*).

Rosa enters and advances on her to chat.

ROSA: So what's new, big sister? (*Settles herself*).

SHARON: Nuttin much (*continues to gaze off*). Nuttin much...

ROSA: Winston gone already? Wh'appen, you two not talking? Who you catch him with this time?

SHARON: Rosa! Lord, how your mind always jump to the worst conclusion like that?

ROSA: Worst? Depends for who, nuh true? Now all like me wouldn't too mind if that happen y'know. I could check for Winston... any day.

SHARON: So I noticed... If you wear your shorts any shorter when he comes by, you will have the breeze cooling where it not suppose to cool.

43

ROSA: Chu, you no see nuttin yet. If me did ever decide to tek weh that one, no problem at all. But no mind yah, sister, I wouldn't do that to you.

SHARON: You really are a little bitch, aren't you? No wonder Daddy can't stand you. You go on, y'see. Not all a the woman who man you sharking going sit back and take it... One a them a go come up here and mark up you face for you...

ROSA: Make them come nuh? They might get to the face, but them could never trouble what I use to tek weh dem men with.

SHARON: Don't bet on it, love. Besides, it seems pretty good for tekking them but it don't seem to be too rusty at keeping dem... if you see what I mean...?

ROSA: (*Annoyed*) Chu... Kenneth was a little saps. Besides, me not wasting my gift on a little nobody like that, me wan' a man, a big man, with some money and a nice car and who can buy me some nice things...

SHARON: An' it no matta if him have one foot and is blind, deaf and dumb. You a something else, bway. Is the first woman I know volunteer to be a piece of beef, even put herself up for sale...

ROSA: Why not? They see and know what they want; I know what I want: business is business and fair exchange is no robbery...

SHARON: So how you sell it? By the pound? Or is it on a lease? Or maybe hire purchase. (*Kisses teeth*). Bway, is one thing when nobody don't value you for yourself, but when you don't value yourself for nothing at all, then you in trouble...

ROSA: Me look like me in any kind of trouble though? You go on. When all like you a sit home a mind baby, all like me a live high...

SHARON: Uhuh. And when all like you old and all the young thing them a trills up you man dem, all like me will have a family.

ROSA: You a saps, bway. Twenty-two and you a talk bout family and love like them things exist any more. Which married man you know don't have outside woman? You want to be the one to stay home and pretend it not happening? You want to tell yourself that you love your husband even though him treat you bad, just because preacher seh you stuck with him for the res' of you life? Not me sah. No way!

SHARON: No, but I tell you something for free. When you and me bucking thirty, forty so, I don't want to be the one all the men are avoiding in public, who sit at home alone if she don't persuade one of them to look for her, who putting on fancy clothes and make-up to try and compete in a race which mekking you into a late nonstarter.

ROSA: Me? A late nonstarter? Me? (*Laughs*). Honey. I'm just too hot to handle, and I don't intend to cool off for now… Besides, nobody don't love nobody any more these days, so why look for something that don't exist.

SHARON: True. And with vultures like you around, how could love survive… Chu, stop it nuh. We have this argument so often I know it by heart. "Men are there to be used. Nobody loves anybody any more, and so on and so on…" Well, you know what, sex pot? I do believe in love. I am a saps. And I hope all like you get burn when you meet someone just as hot as you… (*Sarcastic*) If That Is Possible Of Course. (*She gets up to leave*). Oh, and one more thing, little sister… No bodder trouble Winston. Keep your gravalicious little paws to yourself. Lion? (*She leaves*).

ROSA: Tell you what… let's leave that to Winston, alright?… Well, well, well. Big sister getting serious bout the little saps eh? Wonder if she pregnant… that would be a killing (*laughs*). Papa and Ma would shit up themselves. But chu, she would never do anything so interesting… Life will just go on the same old boring way in this house… boring, boring… BORING. Chu, I could shout till I sick, not a t'ing would happen… wonder if Roy going to call, or Ronnie, or Peter, or Bunny… (*Stretches*). Ah sah, what a life…

Lights down on Rosa preening herself, and smiling, contemplating her conquests.

ACT 1. SCENE 2.

Saturday midday. The scene is set at Errol's yard, or on the doorstep, within earshot of the drawing room. Errol is sitting by himself, talking to himself, thinking. The main conversation starts inside.

MOTHER: Beer: Beer: Beer: All yu do fi di 'ole blastid day is drink dem blastid 'ot 'ops. You can't even drink di beer cool like a big man. Wen you a go stop dis blastid drinkin' and go get yuself a decent wuk?

FATHER: Soon, me will go soon. Me did check wit' Mass Chin but…

MOTHER: Missa Chin? Missa Chin? 'Ow a little shopkeeper a go help you get decent wuk? Yu no tired fi lif' bax and seh 'yes sah' and 'no sah'… You tink a big big manageress like mi a go wan' everybody know seh mi 'usband a wuk inna grocery?… Mi seh fi get likkle ambition an fine a decent wuk fi do…

FATHER: Mi will go look tomorrow, mi love… tomorrow…

MOTHER: Tomorrow? A wah dat good fah? Tomorrow? Fi yu tomorrow nevah come… Di only ting yu ever look fa is beer, beer, beer!

FATHER: But… mi not feelin so good dem las' days yah… Mi head a hot me, a hot me bad…

MOTHER: (*Kisses teeth*) Why yu couldn't be like Mr. Simit'. Him run dat club like a man, 'im is a real man, not a little play play suttin like yu… If yu did dead tomorra him woulda tek me to married right den and dere. All yu can do is sip beer and belch… (*Kisses teeth*). Ah gone go look for Euphemia yah, see wah she haffi tell mi. Mi no wan' see yu in yah so wen me come back… An tell di bway Errol fi go dung a di shop and get some condense milk for mi tea… Mi need it a mornin time…

Mother exits from house and so is first visible. She is a mother young gal, overdressed, buxom and hard-faced. Errol dashes off to hide

46

round the side as she sweeps past and then emerges just as his father comes onto the verandah. He is a small man, who walks a little bent, and is tipsy. Errol looks at him with disgust.

ERROL: Me feel seh you like wen di ole hawg talk to yu like dat. Why the rass yu no tell her fi shut up… you fraid a ar…?

FATHER: Yu shouldn't chat bout wat yu nuh undastan', y'see.

ERROL: Wha fi undastan'?… Dat yu sit down inna di house all day a drink an a seh 'ow yu belly a bun yu, an she go to dat blasted club ebery night fi go rub up on the boss so she woan lose di wuk… Manageress my backside… An' yu let it go on… you siddung pon yu wottless backside an' mek it go on in fron' yu yeye… (*Kisses teeth*). Yu a man doah?

FATHER: I don' see yu runnin' anywhere do… Or yu still a bwoy, an me a di ongle big man round dis yard?… Go on, run up yu mout, yout, but yu know jus' like me dat di day mi get a wuk is di day she chase mi shuttail fram dis yard, an di same fi yu too. Wh'appen to that wuk yu did get ova by di garage fi learn to be mekanic? Tell mi nuh? Eeh?

ERROL: Mi nevah did too wan' fi do dat sort a t'ing… Is nat my breed a wuk dat…

FATHER: What a bwoy lie sah… Yu no even tell di chuth to y'self… Yu no memba wen yu modder come dung deh an' start mek up noise bout 'ow no son a fi ar a go tun no mekanic… 'ow she will fine a wuk fi yu so yu no haffi wear dirty clothes all day… an' ow she tell the boss dat yu did tek di wuk cause yu was too young fi know yu mind properly… Mi no see yu go back round dat side again… mi hear one rass jiving pop round dat side dat day…

ERROL: So? Mi no see yu doing any much betta… Di one dege-dege wuk mi see yu get dung a di Chinee shop she mash dat up fi yu too… Go tell Missa Chin seh him muss'n tek yu on cause you will tief out him tings. (*He starts to laugh at the memory*).

FATHER: Might as well laugh, bwoy, causing dat modder a yours a go keep yu a dis yard until yu ole and ben' and stupid like me…

She a mek di money fi tree a wi and is so she like it... Mi no mind... mi tyad a hackle now... mi will jus' coas likkle while...

ERROL: Mi? Tun like yu? No sah, mi a go dead fus, me tell yu dat fi free. Mi? Yu mad? Just becausen yu no see wah a go on doan mean nuttin a go on my spar... Mi a go on wid more suttin dan yu evah do inna yu lifetime right now and yu would nevah kno till mi personally tell yu... a di chuth.

FATHER: Moretime me did ave mi woman dem a street too; yu not so special... yu jus' likkle younger, das all... Chu, yu full a talk, di day yu do anyting on yu own so me will personally fine a job, tap drink and tell yu modder fi shut up... and mi will tell yu suttin, mi no ready fi wuk again yet. Oh Lord, see yu modder a come deh, look like Euphemia no a she yard mek dem scandalise eberybody... Mi gone, son, mi no wan' deal wid dat piece a miserableness right now... (*Departs in opposite direction*). Oh, an she a bring Munchie wid ar too...

Mother, speaking as she enters with Munchie, a friend of Errol's who is a member of the police force, recently promoted to the CID and working plain clothes.

MOTHER: So how yu enjoying the new line a wuk, Munchie? Yu modder proud a yu nuh...?

MUNCHIE: It not too bad, Missis, and me no haffi wear uniform again so me likkle safer. Dem no shoot yu so quick if dem no know seh yu a police and have a gun dem want to tek...

ERROL: Yu tun detective now, eh? Soon haffi call you Kojak...

MOTHER: Yu father tell yu fi get di condense milk fi mi?

ERROL: (*Ignores her*) So wah yu working on, or you can't talk bout all dat now... Yu catch anybody yet?

MOTHER: But see yah, yu no ha no manners, Errol? Mi ask yu a question an yu no even ha di decency to answered to mi.

ERROL: Come my spar, mek we sit on di step; me tired fi stan near so much noise, it a hut me ears, y'know. (*Goes over to step*).

MUNCHIE: But Errol, yu no hear yu modder…

MOTHER: No bodder try, yah. Is so him facety all di time, tek it fram im fader. Y'see how di Lord send trials to the righteous…

ERROL: A true (*looking at Mother*). A true dat (*implying the trials are his*). (*She turns to go inside*). You mean self-righteous, no so?

MOTHER: (*Kisses teeth*) Munchie, yu modder mus' be a happy woman. (*Goes inside*).

MUNCHIE: 'Ow you treat ar so bad? A no she a feed yu, eh?

ERROL: Chu, if me neva did facety she would a get worried… She need mi and mi fader to be her trial so she can feel seh ar place in heaven guarantee, an di Lord a go pass ova di odder sin dem… It mek ar feel good wen mi facety, and doan a son mus' try fi do wat please him parent, no so King James tell us?

MUNCHIE: Bwoy, sometimes I wish I was like yu, truly, instead of dis blastid wuk. Yu can' leave it at wuk either y'know, if yu a policeman yu a police an' yu cyan figet it…

ERROL: Lie yu a tell, man… yu like di wuk an' me know dat. Wh'appen to yu why yu a talk so…

MUNCHIE: A di odder Sunday man. Chu, mi slip di woman an' go over by Clive house go play some dominoes and tek two waters and so… Mi tell yu, y'kno, we no even sekkle proper to play wen tree likkle yout walk in through di door. An' yu know how Clive place stay already, way inna bush and nobody can see inside the yard, too tough fram di road. Well di yout dem – and is yout fi chue cause the bigges one no reach eighteen yet – dem draw out knife and one a dem 'ave gun… Yu never see hand stretch so high so fas', and mine a reach higher dan the res' bwoy, cause me know seh is all dem likkle young one deh a go kill fi no reason fus, den mek a reason afta… Anyhow one a dem come tek we wallet and watch and mi pretty ring but as dis one a tek, me a watch di one wit di gun cause him neva look too right to me, so him a sway and a shake and him hand well jumpy on the trigger. Him jus' a move the gun fram side to side; so me twitch so him point it at me, so Macky open him mout to seh

49

'beh', him point it at him and im a talk to imself like and smile. But dat no bad… Wen dem done tek all dat now, dem ask a who house dis… Clive him point at Macky, Macky him point at me, me a point at Clive, so the little one wit di gun get red and put the gun long-side a Macky head. As him do so, Macky try hard fi faint him did frighten so. But him couldn't faint… so im head lick him shoulder it straighten back up again, so him straighten up him eye roll ova again and him head pitch down. Anyhow, Clive seh a fi him house and di man leave Macky for a little while. Him tell Clive him mus' cook food for him and him friend cause dem hungry. Mi nearly laugh out dat time, cause if a man no kno how fi cook is Clive. Im could a kill yu before im fatten yu, but so me mek a noise so di gunman swing di gun on me, so Clive go to di kitchen and mi neva seh a word… Likkle more now we all a sit dung pon de floor while di ole criminal a sit in the chair dem a watch we, and Macky start whisper to me: "Oy Munchie, yu a no police, catch dese rass tief nuh…?" Before me a could a tell him im fi shut up one a di yout hear.

"Police? Oo seh police?" and him come closer to Macky. "Yu wan' die young, a talk bout police?" And is the fus' time mi evah see black man tun so white. Anyhow, im brain a wuk now and im seh to di yout…

"Mi? Mi look like me would a wan' talk bout police? Nah sah, mi wus jus' asking Munchie here to puh-lease help Clive wid di cooking cause Clive not di bes' a cook, even when im no frighten." An Macky smile wid di yout till im back teet' a show. Anyhow di yout send mi in to help Clive and mi nearly drop weh mi ston' up cause any'ow dem yout deh did fine out seh me a police, is dead me would a dead today, today.

ERROL: But yu no dead, so nuttin much did happen… Di yout dem get weh?

MUNCHIE: Yu no hear di bes' yet… After dem done eat – and dem eat nearly everyt'ing in di house me a tell yu – dem start rap wid we a little, all play a game a dominoes. Den dem ask fi somebody to drive dem to Spanish Town… Now is only Clive car was there, so Clive seh him will go cause im no figure dem a go shoot him at dis late stage; but di mad one wid di gun, im seh no, im wan' Macky drive dem go… Well bway, dis time Macky faint fi true. Skoy, him jus' lick di floor… Di yout dem frighten y'see, except the one wid di gun, him a laugh. But everybody ben' ova to see if im alright. So we ben', so mi see Clive jus' tek im foot inna im 'and and di' go t'rou di back door, car keys and all. Then me see him draw a halt, tek di car key dem and t'row dem back into the house and then im jump the fence gone. By the time the yout dem see Clive gone and Macky a lie like 'im dead on di floor, dem mussee figure seh it a go get hot, and dem no wan' no police or so come fi dem an seh dem kill Macky, so dem tek we to di bathroom, mek we carry Macky in deh too, and lock we in deh.

We gi dem likkle time fi shif, den we start one piece a shouting. Clive im come back wid some more guys wid lass and ting and dem let we out. No sign o' di yout dem anywhere, dem just missing – we did go look and see, but dem look like dem run gone up the gully or somet'ing. Den wen we coming back to di house, wat we see but Macky a stagger out a di bathroom, ah talk to himself hard hard: "Mi cyan drive sah, is di truth, me cyan drive, do sah, mi cyan drive…" Chu, an if you ever hear Macky talk bout it now, im a hero out deh y'kno. We jus' laugh afta him two time… is pure jive im a go get fram now on.

ERROL: A so di yout dem hard, jus' a walk inna yu house so eeh? Is all like dat yu a wuk on, robbery and shooting and such?

MUNCHIE: Dem no too too like wen we talk bout wat we a deal wid, y'kno… Mi wouldn't mind if it was dat, but a whole heap a different kine a crime and somebody haffi work pon the res' instead a roam street a chase gunman.

ERROL: All like you would have anything to do wid dis rapist guy dem looking for? Is how many, five rapes in the last month and a half, and them still cyan fine nuttin, di papers seh…

MUNCHIE: Him clever, mi will tell you dat… im well clever. Im no go any particular time, im no choose one special type a woman, im tek dem from all area in Kingston. The only t'ing dem know is im alone do it is cause im tie all di woman dem mout…

ERROL: Him do wah… im not too right den…

MUNCHIE: Him no mad if a so yu mean. It mek sense y'kno. Im tie dem mout so dem cyan scream and so, so he can be in a place raping a woman and di neighbour wouldn't hear nuttin fi mek dem suspect… Him well smart… well smart.

ERROL: Jus' cause im tie dem mout, dat don't seem too smart to me…

MUNCHIE: Is not jus' dat… Me feel seh him watch di place dem weh di woman dem live, mussee so, cause the woman dem seh him know where everyt'ing is, and him tell dem wat and wat dem do inna di day… but nobody no memba anyone hanging round di area.

ERROL: But spar, im couldn't rape nobody if'n im no kno weh everyt'ing is… a no chue?

MUNCHIE: Mi no mean so man, chu, you can go on laugh y'see, but me see some o' dem woman deh afta him done wid dem, and dem don't look too nice, mi cyan tell yu… (*kisses teeth*). I don't even know if we can put im in jail afta we catch him cause so we talk to di woman, after di gossip start and eberybody know wh'appen dem no wan't go t'rou no more trial afta dat… and wen di usband and di boyfriend seh dem a go leave di women dem if dem testify and cause more scandalizing and talk, wi cyan fine no-one to tell di court seh him should a lock dung fi life, or go a di madhouse…

ERROL: But it doan look like dem a go catch dis one anyhow, so no problem, mi no figure seh dem a go catch him if im so blasted smart…

MUNCHIE: Smart or no smart im a go get ketch, sometime… no worry bout dat. Me feel seh any man who commit dem breed a crime deh wan' fi get ketch… him no mad exactly but im a play a likkle game like… like a yout who a go on bad cause im want s'mody fi notice im… a so me see it any'ow. But to tell yu di chuth, whoever it is im mussee a hate woman, bwoy. Im do some likkle tings y'kno, like im a show dem seh im is a big t'ing, im a power… Chu, me no come yah fi talk bout dem tings, me come to tell you seh me hear bout one boogie over by the community centre, so mi did wan' know if yu did wan' step so tonight.

ERROL: Dat cool still, me could a listen to two good dub still… oo else a reach?

MUNCHIE: Bwoy, is jus' me and my woman an' yu so far… Yu 'ave a one yu wan' to come?

ERROL: Mi? No sah. Mi one will probe…

MUNCHIE: Still? Yu no fine a woman yet? Or yu no deal in dem tings… (*Errol takes offence*). No, mi neva did mean it that way, guy. Is jus' dat… well… eva since, mi neva see you wid any woman more'n so… All di gal dere, Pauline, she call nuh… she did like you strong, strong, all a call yu baby fader before anyting a go on, but yu run ar…

ERROL: She did a interfere inna mi life, man, so mi tell her fi check out.

MUNCHIE: But yu no ha no life more'n so… me no see yu wid no odder woman no nuttin…

ERROL: (*Looks at Munchie coldly*) Yu memba why me did tell ar fi check out… Aoh. Mi no like nobady, and mi seh nobady at all, interfere in mi life, alright…

MUNCHIE: You different, bwoy, … so me kno… but if a so, den a so… Me nah run no argument wid yu cause you no 'ave no woman, but all di same, mi personally feel seh it no right.

ERROL: What yu a deal wid is dat me no ha woman dat yu kno bout, but no bodder fret bout dat, me deal wid nuff woman.

MUNCHIE: Errol di Mafia… dat cool still, cool… Yu put yu idleness to good use den…

ERROL: Yu could say dat… Doan judge a book by its cover…

MOTHER: (*from inside the house*) Errol, Errol, yu 'ave Munchie out deh a talk to yu so long and yu no offer im suttin to drink… and in di hot sun too.

Errol raises his eyes to heaven. Says nothing. Munchie looks uncomfortable and answers:

MUNCHIE: Is alright… no bodder… mi soon gone any'ow, mi jus' passin t'rou, Ma-am.

MOTHER: No bodder cover up fi him… im a lazy good-for-nuttin… Nobody would ever believe is me bring im up wid me own lov'n hands…

MUNCHIE: Errol. Ah gone. Mi cyan tek di gunfire in dis yard… Mi will call fah yu bout ten-thirty… Tell you fader mi did pass t'rou and miss him… Cool.

ERROL: Yeah… moretime… (*He watches Munchie leave the yard and begins to smile to himself*). Dat deh rapist smart… yu no see smart yet… Mi have couple more well to do, and mi kno seh nobody nah catch mi… That big fat woman in the house who drive di fancy Triumph. A dat mi a go look of to nex… Uhuh… mi betta go ova deh and see wah she a do now… catch who? Mi…? Nah sah, mi smarter than any ole criminal… an mi face too hones' fi s'mody suspeck mi. (*He stretches out, reminiscing and smiling to himself, eyes half-closed. His father comes around the corner quietly and sees him, and stops a while watching him. Errol becomes aware suddenly of his father's presence and jumps*).

FATHER: Wah yu jump so fah? Mi jus' a tan yah a watch yu smile wit y'self… Which woman yu a smile so to tink bout? Eeh?

ERROL: Sneak up like puss, and den yu wan' find out wah me a tink bout… Woman eh-h? Dat a no half a wat me a deal wid fader, not even half…

FATHER: But see yah, is the fus' me see man who no 'ave no money, no job an' no woman so full a 'imself. Mi gone inside to fine a beer, yu want?

ERROL: Nah.

FATHER: Go back to yu dreaming, at least yu look likkle happy wen yu a dream, not miserable like now... Mi gone inside... Yu goin to go get the condense milk fi yu modder?

ERROL: (*Just looks at his father*) Awright, mi will go get it little later.

As his father steps in through the door his mother starts into him. Errol listens a while, then picks himself up to leave the yard.

MOTHER: Is weh yu wus, mi a look fi yu... gone idle down by the bar nuh... well mi feel seh mi nah give yu no more money cause all yu do with it is buy beer, beer and more beer... Why you doan do like Mr. Simit', mi neva yet see him a...

ACT 1. SCENE 3.

The Williams' home again. Eveningish. Mrs. Williams and Rosa... sitting peacefully on the verandah of the house.

MRS. WILLIAMS: So how are things coming at school?... You still having trouble with accounts?

ROSA: Yeah, but no big thing... I figure it won't be my accounts but my statistics that will get me the job I want.

MRS. WILLIAMS: You full of yourself eh? Just pay attention to your classes, because sometimes your statistics, as you call them, won't help you...

ROSA: Is alright Ma, I'm working fairly hard... but Lord it's boring sometimes, trying to see how fas' you can type and take stupid shorthand. But chu, it's what I wanted.

MRS. WILLIAMS: I don't understand that up to now, y'know. You can draw, and you love to sew and cook and make things, but yet you go and do a commercial course... Why you couldn't do somet'ing more... more... well... more satisfying then?

ROSA: You sound like Sharon. "You must look for fulfilment, achievement". I look round this world a little bit, Ma, and I see where is them girls who run round with the boss and don't too mind getting a few little gifts that his wife don't know bout, they are the ones I see getting on in this world. I have no intention of sitting down and waiting for Mr. Right in some little job that only give enough pay to give you worries… No way, no matter how I haffi do it, I going to live the good life. And to find it I going to get a fancy job in one a them big pretty offices with their fancy uniforms and the boss with all the money…

MRS. WILLIAMS: Rosa, Rosa, how you can talk like that… Is as if you father and I never gave you anything…

ROSA: No, Ma, don't think that… Jus' cause I'm miserable and so sometimes… is not you, is me… I impatient. I see the good life leaving me, I see the way society is going now, soon nobody will be left to show me life like I want to live it… It's funny, but I feel like I have to hurry, do everything soon, like maybe I will feel happy if I do that… I don't know, Ma, is a funny feeling.

MRS. WILLIAMS: Rosa, I can't say a word to you, truly. If things were like when I was young, I could tell you you doing wrong… but things have changed so much, so much. I could never do what you are doing, but I can't see a good reason to stop you… (*Sighs*). But love, you can do me a favour…? No, two favours.

ROSA: Like what, Ma? I don't want to make any promises I can't keep…

MRS. WILLIAMS: The first one y'see… I want you to promise me that you will make sure with whatever you're doing, that you feel happy doing it: Don't bother to let any situation force you to do anything you don't want to, alright?

ROSA: That sounds cool, Ma… Now what is number two?

MRS. WILLIAMS: Rosa… Y'know, I watched you and your sister coming up… and even though you younger than Sharon, you stronger than her. So… and don't bother to tell me I am mad either, cause I've thought about this a long time… you must look after Sharon, help her… just be a big sister to her…

ROSA: Ma, I don't really know about that one, tell you the truth… Sharon's too idealistic for me, like she doesn't know the reality of the situation…

As Rosa is saying this, Sharon enters

SHARON: Who don't know the reality of the situation? Who you two chatting about now?

ROSA: You move quiet, boy… I neva even hear the gate move…

SHARON: It was open… So what you chatting about now?… I can hear?

MRS. WILLIAMS: Just passing the time, love. How was work today?

SHARON: Oh… you changing the subject on me, too… Come nuh, jus' tell mi nuh…

ROSA: We were talking about you, since you so fas'.

SHARON: My ears don't burn for nothing. So which reality don't I know?

MRS. WILLIAMS: Sharon dear, it was just a general discussion…

SHARON: Protecting me again, mother…? It wasn't a bad day at work, and I have something to talk to you about, and what reality?

ROSA: Look like you have to change your mind bout dis one, Ma. She persistent if nothing else… Is I was telling Ma that I don't figure you know what is happening in JA now; you still living in a land of principle and people who obey laws…

SHARON: I live in the same world as you, love. But I just see it different from you. I figure that laws are broken all the time, but that don't mean that I haffi do it too… I know that man and woman mash each other up all the time, but that doesn't mean

I have to put myself in the way of getting mash, or cause anybody else to get hurt either… I'm not so sure what I want from this life, but know for sure it isn't that kind of life… You can call me old-fashioned, fool-fool, anything you like, but I not turning another pussy vendor, thank you.

MRS. WILLIAMS: Sharon! There's no need for that kind of language…

SHARON: So Rosa, who don't know the reality now?

ROSA: Chu, Mama has her own reality… the house, Daddy, the supermarket – and me, I have my own too…

SHARON: Yeah. Carl and Junior and Bunny and Robbie and…

ROSA: I can think of much worse ones, sister dear, believe me…

SHARON: I do, sister dear, I do, but not for me…

MRS. WILLIAMS: You two sound like you turning intellectual on me… What you wanted to talk to me about, Sharon?

SHARON: It was you and Daddy actually, but I can tell you one and done… I'm moving out…

MRS. WILLIAMS: What??

ROSA: Say wah??

SHARON: Out. Leaving. Moving… I am moving out.

MRS. WILLIAMS: But Sharon, you can't… I mean, why? For what reason? Where? With whom?

SHARON: Hi! You going on like I no reach twenty-one yet… You can't stop me, Ma.

MRS. WILLIAMS: But Sharon, why? You have your own room here, and you don't argue with anybody…

SHARON: Ma, I am twenty-two, a big woman, and I want to live…

MRS. WILLIAMS: No. I do not understand… and I never will. Time enough when you get married to move out, but alone… alone now.

ROSA: Alone? You sure bout that? How Winston come into this?

MRS. WILLIAMS: Sharon, you're not going to live with him…?

SHARON: Y'see how bad-mind spread?… Is Rosa mention Winston, so you take it onto you head to believe that she know something…

MRS. WILLIAMS: No, no. I didn't mean anything… But why Sharon? You still haven't told me!

SHARON: I did tell you, Mama, except you weren't listening. I said I wanted to live on my own, have my own yard… to live alone… Clear?

MRS. WILLIAMS: You really know what you doing though, Sharon? Paying rent, cooking and cleaning for yourself, you one in there… Suppose somebody break in, rape you, shoot you… you really know what you going to do?

SHARON: Ma, if I listened to all the stories bout gun and rape and such I would never even leave the house to go to work, much less… Lord, Ma, if they coming to trouble me here or there, it don't really matter… I know, I know what can happen. I not pretending that those things don't bother me, but Ma, I just know that I have to get out… I not leaving you, just finding my own home, you understand?

MRS. WILLIAMS: No. I do not understand… and I never will. Time enough when you get married to move out, but alone… in these times… I'm going to get your father to talk to you right now… (*She goes inside*).

ROSA: But how you turn big and bold so? You really going to live alone though? Winston a go live with you, nuh so?

SHARON: Is me one going, Rosa, me one. But is because of Winston, yes. Chu, we can't even find time together anymore. Mama she waits for us if we go out and turn on the light as soon as the car bruck the gate… and his house is no better… and I really want to live by myself now. This Mama and Daddy business getting on my nerves… They always into my skin

"When am I going to get married? Winston is so common… what about Trevor, he was such a nice young man, why don't I invite him over…" Chu, I just want a little space in my head to think, y'know. Sometimes I wish I was like you, Rosa, you don't mek anything bother you. If they don't like what you doing, tough! You going to do it anyway… I can't do that… I just can't.

ROSA: The best is yet to come though. When Daddy hear bout this, hell a go pop in this house… But wait, you find somewhere to go though?

SHARON: Yeah. I rented it from last week, to move in on the weekend. The rent kinda steep, but I figure I can manage…

ROSA: Well, if you can't, you can always get Winston to help… if you can get any money out of that one…

SHARON: True. Lord, hope Daddy don't go on too bad. Chu, I all rented the place and everything already, so why him can't just shut up and leave me alone… Anyhow, I suppose nothing comes easy. True Rosa…?

ROSA: I don't know… some things come easier than others… Lord, Sharon, it was meant to be a joke. Wha'appen…

SHARON: Sorry… Lord, hear Daddy coming now… Wish me luck.

ROSA: Luck fi wah?… If you going, you going, him can't change that… and if the rent paid already, you jus' haffi hope that him settle down as soon as possible and don't sulk too long…

Mr. Williams comes onto verandah.

SHARON: Daddy, did Mama tell you…

MR. WILLIAMS: Yes, she did. I want to ask you some questions right now, young lady…

SHARON: Lord, Daddy, don't argue with me…

ROSA: She's paid the first month's rent already, y'know…

MR. WILLIAMS: I said I had some questions… No need for both of you to jump at me like that… Sharon, have you found a place?

SHARON: Uhuh. In Havendale. It's a flat in somebody's yard.

MR. WILLIAMS: You sure you can afford the rent?

SHARON: Yes, Dad. I think so.

MR. WILLIAMS: Think so? We're not going to welcome you back too too happily if you go and have to come back because you can't afford it. You know that…?

SHARON: Daddy, I can pay the rent; the people are nice in the yard; the flat has burglar bars and if I scream a whole heap of people will hear me… There is a supermarket nearby and the bus runs near the road I live on… I know how to cook and clean and I will have to learn how to wash… I'm not going to have any man living there with me, and I am not going to disgrace you and Mama by any wildness, awright?

MR. WILLIAMS: (*Laughs grudgingly*). You have checked it out thoroughly though… it doesn't look like I have much to say to you… (*He turns away and then turns back to her*) except… (*shyly*) we're going to miss you…

SHARON: I'll miss all of you too, don't worry bout that. But I have to go…

MR. WILLIAMS: Y'know, I can still remember when you two were little and all you had to worry about was homework and pretty clothes… Time passes so fast… so fast…

ROSA: Lord, the two of you look like you trying for "Saps of the Year"… She only going to Havendale… you talking like she going away forever…

MR. WILLIAMS: And don't *you* bother get any big ideas about going anywhere. You have a couple more years in this house to teach you a little sense before you going anywhere.

ROSA: True? I could leave this house tomorrow if I wanted…

MR. WILLIAMS: And be back the day after… Either that or bring so much disgrace to your name that your mother and I wouldn't want to own you...

ROSA: I don't mind, jus' so long as I'm living the good life.

MR. WILLIAMS: Good life? You know good life from bad life though? You still thinking with you anatomy. The day you start to think with you head is the day you are free to go anywhere and do anything with my blessing...

ROSA: Funny how my anatomy smarter than your whole head!

MR. WILLIAMS: Smart? Smart?... With a brain like yours?

ROSA: See, now he says I have a brain... Which one of us don't have any sense...?

MR. WILLIAMS: I have all the cents, that's why you not leaving this house until I say so...

ROSA: Yeah? Well, just watch me...

Sharon watches them in amusement, and turns to go inside, saying to herself:

SHARON: Business as usual today, boy...

Lights down on squabble.

ACT 1. SCENE 4.

Errol's yard again. He is sitting reading a Star *when Munchie comes in.*

MUNCHIE: Ah oh. So yu stay 'ome today... Ah t'ought yu said yu would a check me when yu find out bout dat t'ing fi mi.

ERROL: Mi pass by yu yard one time but yu modder seh yu was at work so mi slide on...

MUNCHIE: Yu too lie, man. Mi check wid di ole lady if yu come an she seh di las' time she see yu was couple months back... Anyhow, yu check you friend fi mi?

ERROL: Yeah, mi aks im but im no really wan' sell di car. Im seh him jus' done fix it up and it a run sweet so im no ready fi sell it yet… but yu could no get one a dem car inna di auction yu people 'ave fi di stolen cars dem? 'Ow you so anxious to spend extra money so?

MUNCHIE: Mi look at di car dem, but chu, mi wan' nice pretty little Mini, not dem big ole ugly sintin… Anyhow, mi cyan really afford one in dis yah hard time, is jus' wan' mi wan' it… Bwoy, it look like if mi no get it now me a neva own a car, much less drive it fi now… but chu guy, yu no fine a wuk yet? 'Ow you spend so much time a walk street and yu no fine nuttin yet?

ERROL: Wuk 'ard to come by, my son, and mi no too wan' tun police mek s'mody kill mi off cause im no like mi face. Beside, me a do a likkle t'ing, y'kno.

MUNCHIE: Anyt'ing in di *Star*? Mi so busy today mi no even see a *Gleaner*.

ERROL: Nah. Jus' politricks and gunman. Same as always… oh and a community protest bout a broken drain… One t'ing me notice tho'…

MUNCHIE: (*He is now looking through the* Star) Uhuh? What dat?

ERROL: Check page two… Yu no see di rapist deh strike again…

MUNCHIE: Yeah, but im only on page two dis time, him not on front page again… Dem a get tired a im now…

ERROL: Dem still don't catch im yet, doah. Yu guys nah do nuttin to fine him?

MUNCHIE: Yeah, mi 'ear one a di officers a seh dem have a clue… Figure im live in dis area someweh cause'n im drop a bus ticket dat buy from 'ere las' time… but chu, is mint a man live in dis area still.

ERROL: Dat no much to fine a man wit. But chu, me figure seh dis guy wan' s'mody catch him, a drop bus ticket and mek di woman dem see im… Im getting slack.

MUNCHIE: Uhuh. But is funny… It look like him a choose di uptown areas to work in now… The last three were in Meadowbrook and Havendale around dere. Mi hear dem seh di big officers tink is a man who was gardener round dere cause im kno di area well… but mi no too follow dat, cause yu jus' haffi walk street to know a place, yu no necessarily haffi work dere, no true?

ERROL: But Munchie, if I was the rapist, me would a do the same, y'kno. Cause wa, im mek di police tink im a move all ova town, den, bam, im stick in one area… Everytime im strike di police figure im a go move on of to dis, so dem no too figure im goin stay in dat area… so di more dem watch fi im, is the more im get away.

MUNCHIE: Dem all have special patrols round dere, plain clothes and everyting… but di trouble is some of di guys dem no tek di wuk too seruss. Dem figure seh di woman dem wan' im fi come in is why nobody never 'ear any noise, so dem no too watch fi im. Dem wan' go chase gunman…

ERROL: Mi would a go back in deh, man, and jus' fine a nice likkle ting, one a dem gal deh who live in one a dem flat, with them stereo and wat, and jus' rape er, yes.

MUNCHIE: Yu too idle, y'see. A talk bout rape like you know anyt'ing bout it. Go fine y'self a decent wuk, bwoy, and stop read *Star* and play domino. How yu so interested in this guy, anyhow? Yu no ask mi bout him di las' time mi did yahso?

ERROL: Is idleness, yes? Mi a read too much *Star*. Mi like di guy style, das all… Anyhow, Munchie, 'ow yu and yu woman a go on? Wen yu a go married? Mi could a well do wit some nice black cake.

MUNCHIE: When dem a give out stubbornness, my girl get nuff a it. Mi a tell you, Errol, is like me and she have agreement like… We a go get married some time, but not right now, me not ready fi it. But me well and ready fi a son. She tek up ar bright self and tell mi seh if me no ready fi married, she no ready to have no son. And all mi talk, tell ar seh she betta 'ave it before she too old, she just seh if mi too young to married, mi too young to be anybody baby fadder… as if me no ha t'ree odder pickney out a road a'ready… Chu, she too stubborn, man.

ERROL: But why you don't just pregnant ar and done? Hole ar down and mek she fight yu… or tell ar seh yu a leave ar if she no do it…

MUNCHIE: It no so easy. She a tek di pill and me can' follow ar everywhere to see she no tek it. Yu can see me a folla ar into the bathroom a di stadium? No sah. And mi nah run ar. Mi love ar, is mi woman, and anyow she draw a bigga salary dan me so she no need me no way… Chu, di women a get too bright dem las' day yah…

ERROL: A true.

MUNCHIE: Run yu mout, bwoy. Me kno seh right now yu no ha no woman more'n so and me no see yu wid none up to now, so mi figure seh yu a bluff still.

ERROL: An' you know everyt'ing eh? Likkle Munchie who did fraid to ask woman to dance not too long ago… You right you cyan run di woman, she a di ongle one to have yu inna ar bed…

MUNCHIE: A mi woman yu a talk bout. So wi nah go talk bout dis subjec' again. Cool?

ERROL: Cool, my spar. And we no bodder talk about my woman situation neither… cool? Yu finish wid mi *Star*?

MUNCHIE: Long time. Ah gone… (*He gets up to leave, still a little huffed, then turns back*). Oh, mi did mean to ask yu wen yu say it… 'Ow you know seh di woman *see* di rapist? Mi neva tell yu dat, and mi no see it noweh in di paper… 'Ow cum yu start know wat di police ongle jus' fine out, bwoy?

Sudden dark on stage with question still unanswered.

ACT 2. SCENE 1.

Interior of Sharon's flat. She and Winston are there, she in kitchen area.

SHARON: You don't like how ah fix up di place, Winston?

WINSTON: Yeah, man. It look cris'. (*He is over by the wall hanging*). Yeah man, look nice... (*Pulls self away*). But Sharon, I not really stopping tonight... mi ha some business to look to.

SHARON: Chu Winston, yu said yu were coming for di evening. Me all cook dinner fi you and all...

WINSTON: Sorry y'hear, love. I tried to get yu at work today but you weren't in the office.

SHARON: So why yu neva jus' leave a message. Chu man, and I could a go to movies with Rosa if ah did kno...

WINSTON: Somet'ing urgent come up, man. Yu no kno by now me wouldn't spoil up yu evening fi nuttin... Chu, shame, Sharon.

SHARON: So what yu come for den? Bwoy, it seem like di only time mi see yu dem las' days is wen you want to borrow di car... Is wah yu would do if Daddy neva gimme dat ole Volkswagon, I don't know... yu drive it more dan mi.

As she comes out of the kitchen he goes to hug her.

WINSTON: How yu so bad-tempered tonight... mi will come for di dinner anodder time... and stay of to dat, too...

SHARON: Yu full a chat. Anyhow, what yu wanted to ask mi?

Winston: See yah, mi a try romance di woman and she a talk so hard to me. Yu know dat is only cause me a wuk up dis t'ing with the recording studio why me a borrow di car so much... If mi get the distribution deal mi will a earn likkle more... maybe even stop spin disc a dat club and work a day time like di res'a people...

SHARON: You still don' tell me wah yu want, sweet boy...

WINSTON: Who seh me want anyt'ing? Any time I come to talk to you is because I want something...?

SHARON: One t'ing or di odder, yes. But serious...

WINSTON: (*Shamefaced*) Ah wan' borrow di car...

SHARON: Uhuh... when?

WINSTON: Aunt Bertha sick... yu remember Aunt Bertha, mi gran aunt? Well Mumma wan' go visit ar so mi sey mi would ask you fi borrow di car... Doctor phone and seh she looking kind a shaky... so...

SHARON: Chu, I wanted to go beach that Sunday too... Anyhow, the place need a dusting, so might as well do it then... Awright (*sighs*) borrow it nuh...

WINSTON: You cool, dawter. Mumma will thank you. I gone now, is only that ah come to bother you wit... You coming to pictures wit me tomorrow afternoon? Is a Clint Eastwood.

SHARON: Alright. I'll pick yu up bout four, okay... (*Winston gets up*). Oh. Winston...

WINSTON: Yeah...?

SHARON: If mi find out seh Mumma measure : 36 - 24 - 36...

WINSTON: You really don' trus' me.

SHARON: Of course I do, love. But to do wat, that is the question...

WINSTON: Chu, go borrow di phone and call Rosa and see if she still wan' go pictures… Yu will get too miserable sitting here by y'self. Ah gone…

SHARON: Yeah.

Lights down and then up on same setting.

ACT 2. SCENE 2.

In Sharon's flat. Saturday evening. She and her mother coming in from shopping. Carrying parcels.

MRS. WILLIAMS: Lord, Sharon, how you mean to lend Winston the car? You father gave it to you, not to him… I just don't understand…

SHARON: If I'd known you wanted to go shopping I would have kept it, but he says he is trying to work up a thing with some record people, so…

MRS. WILLIAMS: Where you want me to put these…?

SHARON: Just dump them in the kitchen for now, I'll sort them out later. Lord, my feet are killing me… You think these shoes will be alright for work?

MRS. WILLIAMS: Yes, if you don't break your ankle on them… But Sharon, you've finished fixing up the place… it looks really quite nice…

SHARON: Thanks Ma. You want a drink? All that hassling on the bus kills me…

MRS. WILLIAMS: But Sharon, why did you lend Winston the car?

SHARON: (*Simultaneously*) Why did you lend Winston the car?

MRS. WILLIAMS: Well, why did you? He's such a… a… taking young man… so… adhesive…

SHARON: (*Annoyed*) Just leave him out of it nuh. You come to spend time with me or you come to criticise Winston?

MRS. WILLIAMS: There's no need to snap my nose off, love... Of course I am concerned about my daughter, I'm your mother after all...

SHARON: How could I forget it...? (*Embarrassed*). You want that drink?

MRS. WILLIAMS: (*After hesitation as to whether to take offence*) Yes, please. What you have? I don't want anything strong.

SHARON: (*Going to kitchen*) Just as well, cause all I have to offer you is some good old fashion "wash"...

MRS. WILLIAMS: You know bout them things too... When I was young, we used to have it all the time...

SHARON: Seriously now, Ma, I feel is Rosa you should worry bout... not me.

MRS. WILLIAMS: Rosa? She can take care of herself, Sharon... What a strange thing to say...

SHARON: You think so, Ma? I don't know... I just get a feeling y'see, that for all her badness, Rosa not too happy with herself...

MRS. WILLIAMS: Not happy? I would say she is more than happy with herself. She certainly makes sure everybody sees it too...

SHARON: That's exactly what I mean. Why does she do that... why she has to dress like that and have so many men around her all the time...? Is as if she don't know what to believe about herself, so she looking for somebody to tell her all the time how wonderful she is... and when there is nobody there, she does the job for herself...

MRS. WILLIAMS: Sharon... you make Rosa sound like she is quite mad... As far as I am concerned she can look after herself a lot better than you can... Oh Lord, Sharon, I'm sorry, I didn't mean it like that...

SHARON: Didn't you, Ma? (*Withdraws*) … Your lemonade alright? I don't like it too sweet…

MRS. WILLIAMS: Fine dear, just fine… (*They both look away around room*). Sharon love, (*tentatively*) is everything alright with you? I mean…

SHARON: Of course it is, Ma… apart from the fact that I can't look after myself, and I have a good-for-notten boyfriend, and I have all the dishes for the past two days to wash and my laundry to do, and I can't afford the pretty dress in the shop we looked at, apart from that I am fine… I don't know what I am afraid of, I really don't. Of living, I guess, and going to work in the morning, and losing Winston, and feeling pain, and…

MRS. WILLIAMS: Sharon!

SHARON: (*Turning impulsively to her mother*) Lord Ma, I don't know what is the matter with me… I really don't… I thought moving out would help and it has a bit, but… and I don't know what to do about it… I keep telling myself it's all in my mind, but I just feel so lost, so alone. So afraid…

MRS. WILLIAMS: Sharon… What are you talking about…? I just don't understand you… What is wrong? You want to come back home and live, is that it? And you're worried about what your father said? My dear, don't worry, come home any time…

SHARON: You not listening, Ma. I said the problem was a little easier since I moved out, not that moving out caused the problem… (*Hopelessly*). I knew you wouldn't understand…

MRS. WILLIAMS: Don't say that, we were so close. Tell me again and maybe I can help…

SHARON: Alright, I'll try, but… it's nothing I can put my finger on, not really… but there is this feeling inside, like there is a blackness there, and sometimes I don't feel anything, nothing at all… not happy, not sad, not anything… and then sometimes I feel it, the sadness, and the darkness growing, feeding on it… Don't look at me like that, Ma, I'm not mad…

MRS. WILLIAMS: And what are you afraid of? You said you felt afraid?

SHARON: I don't know what I am afraid of, I really don't. Of living, I guess, and going to work in the morning, and losing Winston, and feeling pain, and…

MRS. WILLIAMS: Sharon, are you sure you're all right? You know you look a little ill, pale. Why don't you come home with me and have some coffee and chat… it'll be light until we get there if we go now, and your father can drop you back later if you like, and we can sit and chat in the kitchen just like we used to…

SHARON: Lord, Ma, I need to talk now. I don't need coffee and gossip… (*Knock on door*) Oh Lord, who is that now… can't be Winston… I didn't hear the car… Who is it? What? I can't hear you?

MRS. WILLIAMS: You see, you have a visitor… I better be going…

SHARON: But I'm not expecting…

She opens door and Rapist forces way in. Sees mother and puts knife behind back. Signals Sharon to be quiet.

MRS. WILLIAMS: This was my parcel nuh, the rest are yours. I'll just put the meat in the fridge before I go. (*She goes to kitchen*).

SHARON: (*Whispers*) Who are you… I said who are you?

MRS. WILLIAMS: What did you say dear?

SHARON: Not you, Ma. I'll walk you to the bus stop, okay?

Rapist threatens with knife at the words.

MRS. WILLIAMS: Nonsense dear, I'm not that old yet… Besides hadn't you better entertain your guest…? (*Takes her aside*) Who is he? You do seem to have some strange-looking friends… but my love, does Winston know about him? Not that I think you should tell him everything you do, y'know, but… well there is a right and a wrong way to do things if you follow me. (*Glances at rapist*). But he's not that bad-looking really, y'know, a much more honest face than Winston's… Lord, I'm keeping you from talking to your friend… I'm gone y'see… Do call me tomorrow and we can talk some more… Bye, (*to rapist*) nice to have met you… Sharon love, remember what I said…

SHARON: (*Going after her*) I'll just come with you…

The Rapist grabs her back inside.

SHARON: (*Up against closed door*) What do you want from me…? (*Rapist brings knife up so she can see it*) You've come to steal… I don't have much… an old radio and some jewellery. Shall I go get them for you? (*She makes as if to go for them; he keeps her pinned against the door*). Oh… money. That's it, isn't it, you want money…? I don't have much; it's in my purse… (*Indicates purse at other side of the room*). Over there, you see it, on the chair. (*Again tries to go for it; he still keeps her pinned*). Then what do you want? (*Panic in voice rising*) You want food… I just bought some, I even got some fresh chicken… I'll cook it for you, I make a good fricassee chicken… (*He brings knife up to throat*). No. No. Please don't… What have I done to you? What do you want? I'll give you anything I have… but I don't have anything else… (*Rapist begins to crack a smile*). Nothing else, just… (*She cringes away from him, shaking her head*). You don't look like that kind, I mean… you look too kind (*he flashes knife*) no, too intelligent for that sort of thing… I once had a friend who looked like you, a very nice guy, played football, was even on the Jamaica team… same build as you, too… You look like you would be a good footballer… (*Tries to ease away from him as she prattles*) Yes, and you're just the right height too… (*He pulls her closer and starts to put his hand towards her breast*). He was very friendly, too, always trying to back you into a corner, y'know… (*Rapist frowns*), a really nice guy though, really nice… (*She sees tactic isn't working*). Winston and I, y'know Winston? He's my boyfriend, says he coming to look for me this evening, should be here any time now… Well anyway, we went to his friend's club the other night, he just opened it y'know, and the music sounded so good, pure rockers, all night, and he built the boxes himself… uhuh, the big ones were nearly six feet high and you could feel the floor shake when they start to tump… but

Winston says that the tweeters weren't so hot… mid-range is fine, but you need the highs to complete the music, don't you agree…? Anyway, Winston said… Well, Winston don't really know all that much about music… him like rockers though, like Trinity and Althea and Donna and the deejay music… I like them too, roots music… Oh God, aren't you going to say anything… (*She breaks away and he comes after her*) What are you, some kind of machine? (*He grabs her*) Well, are you? If I open you up will I find an engine instead of flesh and blood? (*Rapist looks interested on the word engine*). Well, if you are a machine so am I… I'm a nice little Escort… modified, full of noise and not going anywhere…

RAPIST: You look like a Mini to me.

SHARON: Why? You want to be the Escort…? I mean…

RAPIST: If you cam it up right, Escort will run any a yu fancy car dem offs di road…

SHARON: All like the GTO and the Corvette Stingray…?

RAPIST: Yeah man. Me and my friend a work pon a Ford and we catch one a dem backside at a traffic light, and when we done him haffi pull offa di road… but him sell di Escort…

SHARON: (*Wanting to keep him talking but bucking for a subject*) Ahm… oh… So you work on cars… I have a friend who have a Mini Cooper S who want somebody to help him…

RAPIST: Mi no work pon Mini… is Ford me know bout… Mi love di fas' car dem, don't joke… an y'know how much people have some nice likkle vehicle out deh and no care it properly? Mi see a man bring a nice Fiat 132 into the garage one day, and mi lif the hood and see pure dirt in deh… (*She eases away from him as he talks*) Wen me done clean out dat t'ing y'see, you could a see y'self inna it the way it shine… Chu, if it was all mine now…

SHARON: (*Sitting away from him, trying to appear relaxed*) So what kind a car you would want to drive? I have an old Volkswagon, but it giving me a whole heap of trouble… keep shutting off with me.

RAPIST: Probably the idle want adjus', that's all…

SHARON: No, it's not that, is the distributor, the guy tell me…

RAPIST: Uhuh. Is possible. But you mus' tek wat dem guy dem seh wid a ole heap a salt, cause more time dem jus' want tek di car fi work pon fi strip a part from it… Mi 'ave a friend who could a do di wuk fi yu… but all like you could a neva drive down that side a town all di same…

SHARON: But if you work on cars, how come you not at work instead of…

RAPIST: (*Reminded of why there*) Instead a wat? Eeh?

SHARON: I didn't mean,… I just thought… well work is so hard to come by these days…

RAPIST: Is me you a tell? All like yu don't know bout dis no wuk ting… (*Advances on her again, standing over her where she sits*). But you nevah tell mi why yu tink seh mi come on yah? Why? Tell mi nuh, why?

SHARON: I don't know… I mean, I don't think…

RAPIST: Yu know, yes. Why you a draw way from me so if you no know…?

SHARON: I don't know… (*sobbing*) I don't know, I don't know… I… don't know… (*Curls up, sobbing on the floor*).

RAPIST: (*Uncomfortable at the sight*) Lord… Jus' get up nuh… stop bawl nuh… Mi seh get up… (*He reaches down to pull her up*).

SHARON: Leave me alone, I don't need your help… (*She stands*).

RAPIST: Alright, alright… calm down nuh…

SHARON: Why should I…? You've come here to rape me, haven't you? (*He stares at her*)… Yes, I said "Rape!"… You think I didn't know all along… You think I was talking to you because I liked you…

RAPIST: Stop the crying nuh, woman, you no fe gwan so… behave like a big woman nuh…

SHARON: Wh'appen? You fraid a eye water... Since ah mus go on like a big woman, you don't mind if ah take off the blouse? Is new and ah don't want to rip it...

RAPIST: Mi mine yes... Mi seh stop, leave di button dem... (*Grabs hold of her hand*).

SHARON: (*Quietly, but still almost sobbing*) You come to rape me, that doesn' mean you have to tear up my good blouse... Let go my hand... (*An eye to eye confrontation which Sharon wins*)... Thank you. (*She continues to undo her blouse quietly. He watches uncertain what to do*) Well, is that all there is to it, you watching me undo my blouse, or do you enjoy making you victims sweat... (*She goes back to undressing*).

RAPIST: (*Eventually, after watching in confusion for a while*) Put on back yu clothes!

SHARON: (*Looks up. Pauses.*) Why should... I? (*Looks back down to what she is doing*).

RAPIST: (*Flustered*) Lord gal, mi seh fi put on back yu clothes. Mi nah go trouble you, so do! Just put dem on.

SHARON: (*Looks up at him consideringly, then decides*) Alright. Are you going to leave now?

RAPIST: Mi seh mi nah go trouble yu, mi no seh mi done with yu yet.

SHARON: Oh. So what do you want then... Oh cut that out, you said you weren't going to rape me... What do you want now?

RAPIST: Lord, how you so blasted pushy... Gimme time to tink likkle bit nuh. Chu, yu jus' confuse up mi head, a talk bout car, and a bawl and lie down pon di or... You no ordinary...

SHARON: Would you like a beer...? Cool you off a little before you go home...

RAPIST: Mi seh is mi fi decide weh mi a go do... Shet yu mout and mek big man tink nuh... Chu...

SHARON: Alright. Sorry... (*She sits waiting patiently, disconcerting him further*).

75

RAPIST: (*Eventually*) Jus' bring the beer and done nuh... Sekkle off mi head... Is so you treat yu man, woman... mi would a go mad.

SHARON: How you know seh mi have man anyway? (*Goes for beer*).

RAPIST: Dat no hard fi know... Is ongle whether you 'ave one man or nuff man. Mi only see di likkle brown skin bwoy come on here all the same, you car him a drive...

SHARON: Whole heap a people don't know either... That's Winston I was telling you about...

RAPIST: But mi a watch you long time, and mi know seh you no go out too much...

SHARON: Boy, y'know since me and Winston start up, I don't really go anywhere much... I used to though, y'know, go out and boogie and all that, but I find seh I can't deal with them people and the constant competition them running... Who have on the most expensive outfit, who man buy who which pretty jewellery, who see who at the Pegasus with who boss... Not for me, sah. No way. But y'see, if you don't check fi all dat, you can't find nobody to tour with... and Winston him don't take me anywhere these days...

RAPIST: But dawter, you a well looking beef. Man and man mus' check you out a street...

SHARON: Yeah. A nice beef. Just like yu said. They don't want to know me, Sharon Williams, they want to check dat beef deh.

RAPIST: Oh, is Sharon you name... Mi name Errol. But dawter, you no glad seh you stay so, you would a preffa if di man dem pass yu and no even bodder look pon the structure...?

SHARON: No, is not that... but I want somebody I can deal with, who can talk to me like I can think, can communicate...

RAPIST: But dat no mean seh dem haffi tink too? How much a dem man deh yu figure ever tink a anyt'ing except 'ow fi fool up anodder woman? Most a dem a chase it fi so long, dem vanc di tinking business long time, deh no memba how fi tink...

SHARON: Yu harsh eh…? Is true all the same. I was talking to this guy, a serious serious talk to y'know, and all ah hear is carburettor and cam, tweeter and pre-amp till ah nearly drop asleep… Den him look at me and seh how glad him was to have a meaningful conversation… I was very polite though, Errol, I didn't laugh in his face…

RAPIST: Proud a yu… Is a dread world eeh? When man and man start feel seh other people nuh worth as much as machine, and yu a use who should a be yu friend fe show other people how you bad…

SHARON: Boy, sometimes I feel I not born to this world at all, y'know… I mean it…

RAPIST: Mi nevah seh yu no mean it, mi jus a seh di worl a appreciate that likkle structure still, so you cyan tek it weh…

SHARON: Lord be serious nuh! Is something that bothers me a lot. I try talk to mi sister, and is like me and she live in two different world. My mother don't even know how to handle the changes she going through herself much less help me with mine. And my father – well. I mean ah know I love him, but I don't know him more than so…

RAPIST: But yu no mus ha friend fi talk to? Mi always see unnu office gal a walk and talk togedder like unnu nevah a go stop…

SHARON: You damn right they never stop… and when you walk away from the group is you dem start chatting. No sah, is very few woman I trust to tell my business to…

RAPIST: A true? Is so woman vicious?

SHARON: I wouldn't say vicious, Errol, but from dem born dem modder teach dem that their own kind is the enemy and man is the only thing worth being loyal to… and some of them not afraid to stab up the enemy… Serious though, I look at you guys, how you play football together and drink and laugh and talk, and sometimes I think you are so much luckier…

RAPIST: You feel seh cause man and man laugh together more,

dem backstab any less… Chile, yu not born to this worl fi true…

SHARON: Do, don't tell me that… I need to believe something good about humanity…

RAPIST: But see mi yah…

SHARON: The world turn upside down now. You come here to rape me and now you telling me I must call yu the hope for humanity… What a life!

RAPIST: Well, ahm, if the dawter no too mind, me well hungry an could a do with a small nourishment… The beer inna di empty belly kinda…

SHARON: I don't believe this day… truly. I am sitting chatting to a man who came to rape mi and him asking me if I don't mind getting him something to eat… Madness. What you want? I think is only some bully beef I have…

RAPIST: And you was a talk little while bout chicken…

SHARON: If you had ever let me go prepare it for you, I would a gone through the back door and make the police come and get you…

RAPIST: So you a warn mi seh you a go shif… (*Instantly defensive*) Me will come wid you inna di kitchen mek sure yu no try nuttin… .

SHARON: You really think I woulda do dat…? If you will stay and talk to me, I will fix you a sandwich – that sound fair to you?

RAPIST: Cool, my dawter.

She goes to fix sandwich and he sits in other area.

SHARON: So Errol, this is the first time you never rape the woman? I mean you raped all the others?

RAPIST: None a yu business dat… Mi should a jus' rape you and done instead a mek yu ask mi dem breed a question deh…

SHARON: Chu, how you gwan so? You think is everyday a woman get to talk to a real live rapist? Just tell me nuh man…

RAPIST: What you want to know?

SHARON: Well… I mean… well, why do you do it?

RAPIST: Mi cyan tell you dat dawter, mi no know dat…

SHARON: But you mus' know! Don't you watch the women and choose dem and everything?

RAPIST: Yeah, mi do dat. But mi no know why. Is like mi jus' know seh mi haffi do it fe get likkle peace inna mi head…

SHARON: Peace? (*Coming in with sandwich*) You feel peaceful after you hurt somebody like that?

RAPIST: Wah yu a stare pon mi like dat fah? Yu tink seh me a mad man, don't it…? Well, mi no mad, and mi nah talk to yu again bout it neider.

SHARON: Lord Errol, I don't think you mad… Is jus' that I could never understand why a man would want to… (*There's a knock at the door. Sharon looks at watch*). Oh my God, Winston! Is so time fly… Do Errol, go hide for me nuh…

RAPIST: Hide? Mi mus' hide? Mi nah do nuttin dat mi should a hide…

SHARON: Not you, stupid…! Me. If Winston catch me in here with you, him will…

RAPIST: No likkle middle-class bwoy a go raise im hand to any one a mi friend dem while me deh bout… Open di door.

SHARON: (*Knock again*) Coming! Errol, don't bother start any fight in here please… Coming!

WINSTON: Wh'appen, you can't open de door when I knock… what you doing so that… Oh. Hail sah. I know the man?

RAPIST: Nah.

WINSTON: Di man is a relative of my dawter?

79

RAPIST: Nah.

WINSTON: Ah see. Yu jus' a pass t'roo.

RAPIST: She and me was a rap.

WINSTON: Dat cool still. (*To Sharon*) I could do with a cold beer, y'know. Come get it for mi nuh… (*Leads her off in direction of kitchen*). Is so it go, eh? I leave you at yu yard, tell mi that you going shopping with you mother, and when ah come early you a have man in here with you…

SHARON: Winston, he's not…

WINSTON: I'm sure he isn't… neither am I, to him, I suppose. Woman, bwoy, you can't trust dem one shit… You have yu woman but dat no good enough. She want more dan one man, she mus' have plenty while she argue wid you bout how you have woman a street…

SHARON: Will you jus' listen to me! I said…

RAPIST: (*Taps Winston on the shoulder*) Excuse me y'see, but no yu mi did see by the street dance out by Bayside?

WINSTON: I know you've never seen me anywhere before… Me and my daughter talking y'know… in private…

RAPIST: Yeah man. Mi see… Is just dat las' Saturday dere me know seh mi see you at Bayside. Is cause me memba di car, y'know, and the three uptown ting you did a tour wid… Dem look fit, my brother, well fit…

SHARON: Winston? You said you were taking your mother to Mo Bay that weekend… Your grandaunt was ill remember. You even came back and told me she was getting better…

RAPIST: Him mussee go down that side the Sunday, cause me know me see him a town the Saturday night… Yeah man, I remember the Volkswagon…

SHARON: Well?

WINSTON: Sharon, you going to take that butu word against mine… If I told you I went to Mo Bay I went to Mo Bay…

SHARON: That butu happens to be a friend of mine… and (*pauses*) you know something, I do believe him… and you have an awful lot of explaining to do…

WINSTON: I was just dropping off some of my cousins… Mama didn't want to go down till Sunday because…

SHARON: You told me you didn't have any *girl* cousins… much less three…

WINSTON: Sharon, this is a matter of trust… Do you think I would do a thing like that to you?

SHARON: Yes, I think you would. But you wouldn't want me to know about it, though, now would you… cause then you might not get the car to borrow and the free food, and have somebody stupid enough to lend you money when things get tight.

WINSTON: Sharon, why are we arguing? I'm sure we can settle this alone…

SHARON: In other words, I must tell Errol to leave, so you can sweet talk me… Not this time… not any more…

WINSTON: Sharon, I don't have too much patience with this kind of behaviour from a grown woman…

SHARON: Pity I can't say that you are a grown man… You know who is leaving this place now…? Guess…? And is not Errol…

WINSTON: This is your last chance, Sharon…

SHARON: Get out! Last chance? Last chance to do what? To make up with a liar and a parasite…? I said get out! This is my yard, and I said…

RAPIST: (*Coming back into kitchen*) Di lady said yu fi get out… (*Takes Winston by the shoulder and points him toward door despite his protests*), and mi tink seh she nah joke, y'kno.

WINSTON: Let go of me… Sharon, I warn you, you'll be sorry…

SHARON: (*Quietly*) The only thing that I am sorry about is that I didn't do it sooner… (*She puts hand out for car keys, he throws them on floor and slams out.*

There's a pause.

RAPIST: Well, you nah go start bawl…? Him gone, yu man gone…

SHARON: My man? No sah. I don't share what is mine like that… I meant it, y'know. I should a run him long time… I wonder if is you give me the courage to do it…

RAPIST: Mi? Nah, sah. Is you one do it… me jus' gi yu di reason…

SHARON: That was help enough… You want mi to fix up a next sandwich? Then you can go, cause it getting kinda late and I have to go wash my hair and do the washing up tonight…

RAPIST: Cool, dawter. You have any scotch bonnet pepper fe put inna the bully beef?

SHARON: One bully beef sandwich with scotch bonnet pepper coming up… (*Exits to kitchen as rapist makes himself comfortable*).

ACT 2. SCENE 3.

Errol and Sharon in her flat. Relaxed and talking.

ERROL: So you hear from yu guy again since yu run im las' week?

SHARON: Yeah man, im call nearly most every day at work… tell mi seh him will forgive mi, for disgracing him like that (*laughs to herself*).

ERROL: Him no figure him owe you an apology?

SHARON: No sah. The only t'ing he is sorry about is that him get ketch.… Oh, and that him can't get to use di car again. Mi a drive inna di Plaza las' weeken' an mi see a girl a stare pon di car, den she look pon mi, den she stare at di car again… den her face get vex up… Winston a go ketch him arse from ar, bwoy. Bet yu ar name is Bertha an she well wan' go beach again. Not in this car though...

ERROL: So you fine another guy yet...?

SHARON: Nah. Mi not lookin' so hard, tell yu di truth... Winston kinda shake up mi faith in human nature... Well, man nature anyway...

ERROL: But yu 'ave mi fi show how man can nice...

SHARON: Ah true... but seriously, yu haffi admit t'ings in a bad way when ole criminal a tell mi to cheer up...

ERROL: Who yu a call ole criminal...? Dem no ketch mi yet. Dem nah go call mi criminal till dem ketch mi, an dem nah go ketch mi...

SHARON: Errol, ah know is fas' mi fas', an is none a mi business to ask you, but... ah mean... well, why?

ERROL: Why? Mi nuh know... Wuk 'ard fi come by so mi a learn a trade...

SHARON: No. Be serious. Is a brute of a crime... I went back and read the old reports... You hurt up dem woman bad, y'kno...

ERROL: Of course mi kno. Ah no mi di ee? Chu, stop talk bout it nuh? Mi come 'ere to fine out bout yu, no fi talk bout mi...

SHARON: I heard that you can go to a psychiatrist who...

ERROL: Psychiatrist? A Bellevue? Afta mi no mad man... Is wah yu tryin' to do to mi? Yu a tell mi wah fi do to? Eeh, yu tun like di res'a dem? Eeh? (*He is holding her by the shoulders and shaking her as he talks louder and louder*).

SHARON: Sorry... I said sorry... Lord Errol, let me go, mi neva mean to fas'... do Errol...

ERROL: (*Lets her go*) No bodder fas' inna mi mine again... Mi no fraid fi yu... so no trouble mi...

SHARON: Fraid a me? Wat reason you could have to be fraid a mi? Errol! Errol! (*He has gone to the other side of the room and is staring at the wall*) You want to talk… let me jus' go get a drink fi yu and we will sit down and talk… Alright.

She goes into the kitchen. He picks up a piece of cloth lying nearby (a blouse? dishcloth?) and walks up behind her. Just as she turns to bring the beer back into the room he puts the rag over her mouth. She struggles free, but he eventually puts the gag into her mouth.

SHARON: See di beer… Jesus Errol… Errol…

ERROL: (*Gets out his knife*) Tink yu a friend a mine eh? A bring mi beer to drunk mi and mek mi tell yu wat yu want to 'ear… Well mi nah talk, mi nah list'n to yu a try to help mi… Mi and mi friend no need no help from nobody… y'hear mi… nobody… (*He pushes her into a chair and stands over her. Brings knife near her face*). Uhuh. So mi wan' yu to look scared… yu fi fraid a mi, yu nuh fi tell mi wah fi do… (*She makes as if to run*) …Mi seh siddung… Weh yu goin'…? Mi and mi fren nuh done wid yu yet… Siddung mi seh… Yeah, cry nuh… mi a go mash yu up. (*Voice is very low*) Mi mus' fetch yu condense milk? Mi mus'n wuk as no mekanic? Mi mus' seh anyt'ing yu tell mi fi seh…? Uh-uh it no go so no more… mi a di king, mi… mi… mi… Weh dat beer bokkle deh… (*Sharon screams behind the gag and he goes over and switches on her radio and turns it up full blast*) …Go on, scream nuh…

Sharon dodges past him, he catches her and pulls her slowly back to him with the beer bottle held in front of her eyes. She is terrified; Errol is grinning wickedly. She breaks away and Errol grabs after her and her skirt comes off. He forces her into the bedroom off-stage. Screams, shouts, slaps, etc. Lights down.

ACT 2. SCENE 4.

All set in Sharon's flat. In one evening, the day after the rape. Rosa and Sharon are alone.

SHARON: Lord Rosa, do. Fix yu face… mi no dead yet…

ROSA: Sharon (*She comes over and embraces*). Sharon, you alright…? Yu feeling better? Mama and Daddy soon come. Mi did get one a di people at di office fi drop mi yah… Why you didn't call us last night?… Jesus Christ, Sharon…

SHARON: Do. Mi no feel like too much fuss and bodder round mi now… All I feel for is a bath…

ROSA: But yu jus' come out a di bath…

SHARON: Mi feel dirty, nasty… right down inside a mi… I feel… unclean.

ROSA: But Sharon, what happened? I mean… well… what happened?

SHARON: Jus' what a told yu… I was raped.

ROSA: I know. I know… but how?

SHARON: Rosa if yu don't know what rape is at your advanced age, den you mussee di world's biggest shaper…

ROSA: Is not dat… but… well, I don't think I would a eva get rape… Didn't they always tell yu jus' to sit back and enjoy it…

SHARON: And you believe dat? Yu believe somet'ing as disgusting as dat… Disgustin'… Mussee a man tell yu dat, cause if yu respec' yu body at all yu would neva neva let anybody touch you… touch you… (*Starts to cry, hugging herself*).

ROSA: Jesus, Sharon, ah neva mean to upset yu so… Do Sharon… Sharon! Stop crying… please!

SHARON: Is alright, Rosa, don't upset y'self, is alright.

ROSA: See Mama and Daddy here… Do hush Sharon…

SHARON: Is alright… is alright…

Mr. & Mrs. Williams enter. Her mother rushes over to her on the couch, while her father lingers near the doorway… as if embarrassed.

MRS. WILLIAMS: Sharon… Sharon… I know we should neva have let yu move out… living alone, so young and defenceless… We should neva have let yu…

SHARON: Is alright, Mama. Yu didn't kno it would happen…

MRS. WILLIAMS: But I should have… it happens so often… so often…

SHARON: (*Snaps at her*) And people get killed by cars every day too… If you guilty it makes it easier for yu, but it don't help me none… (*nearly screaming*) it don't help mi one fucking bit, do you hear…

ROSA: Alright Sharon. Alright. Mama never meant nuttin… by it… nuttin at all… Ease up, wi come to help yu…

SHARON: I don' want any blasted help… ah jus' want peace and quiet…

MRS. WILLIAMS: Alright… Rosa, you and Daddy go back to the house, I'll stay with Sharon.

SHARON: No. Ah mean, not tonight, Ma. I'd just like to be alone. I have somet'ing to think about…

MRS. WILLIAMS: I will not allow you to stay here by yourself… so don't argue with me…

SHARON: Ah not arguing with you, Ma, I'm asking yu to go home… Please…

MR. WILLIAMS: (*Tentatively*) Sharon, would you mind if I stayed?

MRS. WILLIAMS: Donnie (*in stage whisper*), she won't want a man…

MR. WILLIAMS: Sharon? I would like to…

MRS. WILLIAMS: Donnie, don't pressure her, she's been through a lot…

SHARON: Is okay, Mama. Yes, Daddy, please stay… I would like that.

MR. WILLIAMS: Rosa, will you drive your mother home?

ROSA: Sure, Dads. Come on Ma… Sharon wants to res'…

MRS. WILLIAMS: Now Donnie, make sure she has something to eat and she is to have one of those pills Dr. Martin prescribed…

SHARON: (*Sharply*) You spoke to Dr. Martin?

MRS. WILLIAMS: Yes dear, of course… I had to find out how you were.

SHARON: Find out how I was, or get all the details to broadcast to your friends…? Eh, which one, Mama? Well, you can tell Rosa all about it, cause she's been dying to know, haven't you little sister…? Oh, get out, just leave me alone… get out… The sideshow hasn't started yet!

Mrs. Williams and Rosa leave, with much headshaking and curious looks. They are quiet as if in a madhouse or hospital.

MR. WILLIAMS: Er-r… Sharon? Come sit down here and talk to me…

SHARON: Not you too, Dad. You want to know the details too?

MR. WILLIAMS: No. I can *see* the worst effect on you already. No. Tell me about you and Winston… He buck me up the odder day and start tell me that you bus' up.

SHARON: Oh God, Daddy, if only I had had a little sense… just a little…

MR. WILLIAMS: But you couldn't have known he wanted to rape you, Sharon.

SHARON: But Daddy. I did! That's the worse part… I knew all along… He has been here three times. It's partly because of him that Winston and I broke up… Daddy, he was a really nice guy.

MR. WILLIAMS: (*Pauses, looking flabbergasted*) I think you better tell me about it…

SHARON: He broke in… to rape me but he didn't… not the first time… and we used to chat a lot… He actually listened to me, cared about mi…

MR. WILLIAMS: But Sharon, you know all a wi love you…

SHARON: No Daddy, not like dat, not like family… He really liked me… me with all mi foolishness… and I liked him…

MR. WILLIAMS: But Sharon, you should have reported dis business to the police long time… And why didn't you tell us?

SHARON: I didn't want to report him… and I couldn't tell you. You would make mi report him, and I didn't want to; it was so cruel…

MR. WILLIAMS: For God's sake Sharon, talk sense. The man raped you… Yu are in pain because a im…

SHARON: That's what I don't understand… Why did he rape mi? I went to get a beer and he came up behind me… started talking about mi sending him to get condense milk and stopping him from being a mechanic and all sort of craziness, then he… then he…

MR. WILLIAMS: I know, love, yu mother told me… Come here… Hush, love.

SHARON: What am I to do, Dads? They're going to catch him, I know it… I didn't describe him too well, but they sounded like they had a good idea who it was… even knew his name was Errol… but Daddy, why? Why did he turn on me like dat? Why? Why he hate me so…

MR. WILLIAMS: I don't want to be upsetting, love, but have you thought about the trial… Ah mean, are yu goin' to testify?

SHARON: I don't know, Daddy. Y'know, is funny but I still feel like a betray him wen me talking to the police… I jus' don' know wat to do… and the police seh none o' the other women dem wan' to come forward at dis late stage and say anyt'ing; dem jus' want figet it and done. Mi figure seh is because dem get such a hard time when people find out bout it… all ova di

Star… Y'kno, Daddy, he was proud dat his rape dem get inna *Star*… Is like di only t'ing he had eva done dat people notice… Lord Daddy, wat a t'ing… Mi nuh kno wat to do, I really don't.

MR. WILLIAMS: I suggest you jus' sleep tonight and tomorrow we will talk it over wit' yu mother and Rosa… I'll stay on the couch with you…

SHARON: Alright, Dads. I'll go have a bath and go to bed… but if I can't sleep, mi can come talk to you again?

MR. WILLIAMS: You tink I stayed to keep myself company? Do, stop worry about all a dis and sleep a good night. Mi within whispering distance… Everyt'ing passes, my child…

SHARON: Yeah. I'll do that… Lord, ah feel tired… to me bones…

Loud imperative knocking on the door. Sharon jumps. Draws her dressing gown around her. Her father goes to answer the door.

SHARON: Who is dat now, Lord? Hope is not the press.

MR. WILLIAMS: Yes… Can I help you?

ERROL'S MOTHER: Ah no yu mi wan' see. Mi come to talk to one Sharon Williams.

MR. WILLIAMS: Sharon isn't feeling too well. She gone to bed.

ERROL'S MOTHER: So she live yah fi true. Is so Errol tell mi. Mi wan' talk to ar. Wake ar up…

MR. WILLIAMS: I beg your pardon? My good woman…

ERROL'S MOTHER: Do, no bother drop on yu fancy accent pon mi… Mi seh mi wan' talk to ar, she an mi 'ave some bisniss to deal wit… 'Oo yu anyway?

MR. WILLIAMS: I am her father. And she is not goin' to see anybody tonight, you could be Jesus modder herself, you not coming in here.

ERROL'S MOTHER: Mi no fraid fi mek up noise an' go on bad, y'kno, so jus' step one side, mek me talk too 'oo mi come to talk to…

MR. WILLIAMS: You neva hear wat mi seh… mi seh…

SHARON: Is alright, Daddy, mek her come in… She a push in anyway, so mek her come in…

ERROL'S MOTHER: Yu dawter a more sense dan yu… (*She sweeps past father who follows her in and continues to hover protectively*). Yeah, is yu mi wan' deal wid…

SHARON: You seh Errol told yu where to fine mi… How you know Errol?

ERROL'S MOTHER: Mi nuh mus' kno im… afta im a mi son…

SHARON: Your son… I didn't even tink of im as havin' a mother…

ERROL'S MOTHER: So 'oo you tink keep im…? Him not even workin' any money an im get arres'… an is mi one a go haffi help him since im fadder no worth nuttin neider.

SHARON: But why would Errol send you here?

ERROL'S MOTHER: Well, im never really sen' mi strickly, but ah figure seh mi could a reason wid yu still an mek yu see likkle sense…

SHARON: Sense…? Like what?

ERROL'S MOTHER: Mi was talkin' to one a im fren dem a di station… an im tell mi seh yu a di one key wickness cause di odder woman dem no wan' tan' up in court and talk bout wat did 'appen… even di one dat did see im no wan' seh nuttin cause ar husban' seh im a go lef ar if she go a court an get ar name into *Star* again… Anyhow Munchie tell mi seh…

SHARON: Munchie? But dat is his good good friend. Munchie a policeman?

ERROL'S MOTHER: Yeah man, is Munchie figure out dat is Errol do it… Im neva kno waffi do, so im telephone mi a mi wuk-place, seh mi mus' tell Errol im in trouble, den im tell the office dem wat im figure out… Y'see wat a mean, di blastid boy good for nuttin. Before im jus shut him mout an do wat im a do, im a go tell Munchie likkle bit likkle bit so, if an a but, until im figger out is im do ee. Any'ow, mi no come yah fi talk bout dat. Mi come fi tell yu seh it don' suit yu to testify gainst mi son.

SHARON: But how come if him so wuthless yu no wan' im to go a jail?

ERROL'S MOTHER: Im could a go a jail yes, but mi 'ave mi reputation to t'ink bout and me no too sure seh dem would a wan' a manageress at di club 'oo son a rapist... Mi haffi proteck miself.

SHARON: Protect y'self...? Jesus Christ, yu no undastan' eh? Yu son a rapist... im rape woman... yu no undastan... woman like you... like me!

ERROL'S MOTHER: Like yu, baby, no mi. Nobody nah go trouble mi. Chu, me feel seh all a dem woman enjoy it, das why dem no wan' talk up in no court... Is my son afta all...

SHARON: I just can' believe wat I am hearing... Enjoyed it...? Enjoyed it...? Does anyone enjoy being beaten up, robbed, humiliated? Enjoy it... My God!

MR. WILLIAMS: You want me to get rid of her?

SHARON: Is alright, Dads. I want to kno why she come at all...

ERROL'S MOTHER: Yu no mus' kno mi a come tell yu seh mi 'ave a likkle money put aside... If you don't seh nuttin at the trial mi will gi yu. If yu wan' testify, yu can go on to, but it might be not such a good idea if yu wan' fi stay healthy, y'undastan...?

SHARON: Yeah, mi undastan... mi undastan... You don't care fart for Errol but yu no want nobody seh yu 'ave son dat a criminal... Mi undastan, lady... Yu a go pay yu good good money so no scandal no reach yu.

ERROL'S MOTHER: No bodda tun up yu lip afta mi... Yu kno anyt'ing bout wat is like to get somewhere in dis worl widout anybody 'elping yu? Wat is like to haffi struggle an support two wutless man?

SHARON: But Errol said he had a job in a garage...

ERROL'S MOTHER: Garage? My son fi go wuk inna dut and grease... Fi wah? Nah sah, mi go dung a di garage and tell di big big manager dat mi son too good fi all like im. Mi son mus' be somet'ing in dis life, not a –

SHARON: ...mechanic... Now I understand... (*Quotes Errol*): "Mi mus' fetch yu condense milk? Mi mus'n wuk as no mechanic? Mi mus seh anyt'ing yu tell mi fi seh." Daddy, that's what he said to me... jus' before... (*She starts to laugh*). Y'kno somet'ing... Errol wasn't raping me... he was raping you... you... You pushed im aroun and im couldn't seh nuttin so im rape to tek out im anger... Jesus... poor ting.

MR. WILLIAMS: Sharon, he raped you... remember dat... Wah yu haffi think bout right now is if yu going to testify or not... Look, mi know yu haffi decide... but do, please tink about di fuss and scandal dat a go follow yu name, especially wen his lawyers fine out dat he come here before...

SHARON: Wh'appen, Dads. (*Bitterly*) You fraid fi scandal too... I know... I'm sorry... I know how it's goin' to be, don' worry; a girl at the office got rape las' month and she no settle down yet. Everytime she walk into the canteen, them seh: "Yes, that's de one. Is she get rape." And the jokes about how a woman can run faster with her skirt up than a man wid his pants down... Y'kno rape mus' be the only crime when the victim suffer more than the accused in court... Wat they call it... me see it on television all di time... character assassination... somet'ing like dat anyway... I don't know, father. It look like yu and dis old bitch a sing di same tune... Mi no kno...

ERROL'S MOTHER: A bet a thousan' dollars will 'elp yu kno tho'...

MR. WILLIAMS: If my daughter decides to stay silent, it will not be because of you blasted thousand dollars...

ERROL'S MOTHER: Chu, yu was a chat sense likkle while, but yu tun fool again now. Mek di gal mek up ar mine... Mi no ha all night neider, cause mi haffi get to wuk before dem gal deh start bad-mout me bout dis ting... Yu wan' di money or not?

MR. WILLIAMS: People will make life hell for you… gossip…

There's a knock at the door.

MR. WILLIAMS: Is who dat now… I hope this is pleasanter than the last visitor… (*He glares at E's mother as he goes to the door*).

MUNCHIE: Miss Sharon Williams, please…

MR. WILLIAMS: Who are you now? And wat do you want?

MUNCHIE: Police, and I want to talk to Miss Williams about a personal matter…

ERROL'S MOTHER: Munchie, wat yu a do yah… yu follow mi?

MUNCHIE: (*Entering*) Yu wuk fas', boy. Errol seh yu would try to talk to Miss Williams… How much yu offer ar?

ERROL'S MOTHER: Shame on yu. A boy like yu dat mi know since short pants a come point finger at me like me a criminal too…

MUNCHIE: Errol talk to me… Him seh him want mi to talk to Sharon… I mean Miss Williams. He give me a message (*turning to Sharon*)…

SHARON: Message? To me? The man who rape mi sendin' message to mi… What a night, sah… Confusion, and ah so tired, too.

MUNCHIE: Him tell mi it was urgent. Him did wan' mi get 'ere before im modder, but the old bitch crafty bad… no true…

ERROL'S MOTHER: Is wits why mi stay alive so long, and is wits why mi a go stay alive till mi ninety…

SHARON: So wat did he say?

MUNCHIE: Well, him talk to him lawyer and him find out seh (*Errol's mother is coming closer to listen, so Munchie draws Sharon aside*). Come mek we talk ova here. Yeah, im fine out seh im can get treatment and get likkle time to think and see if im really mad, so im seh you mus' testify…

ERROL'S MOTHER: (*She has crept closer and hears the end*) Is lie: Errol no wan' go to no prison at all... Is lie im a tell, im a policeman im a trick yu...

SHARON: (*Very angry*) Y'kno, me a go testify afta all... an yu kno why? Cause mi like yu son... Im hurt mi and I still hole a hatred in me heart for dat... but mi see now weh it mighta be di bes' t'ing all round if me jus' send him to prison one time and see wah 'appen. Mi don' see how he could be much worse off if he stayed with you... If im no go mad in jail, im would a go mad wit yu aroun' im. So is might as well mi sen' im dere, cause at least he cyan trouble nobody in dere, an' he will be safe from yu and yu wickedness...

ERROL'S MOTHER: Wickedness? Mi? Mi feed im and clothes im an mek im go school... And you humiliated him and shamed im wid yu loud mout and bossiness... But see yah, dis likkle brown rass come to tell mi wah mi fi do wit mi one son... A fi mi son and no little bitch a go put im in jail and mash up fi mi life... y'hear mi!

SHARON: Yeah, im a your son, like yu vanity a yu vanity, and yu ches' a drawers is yu ches' a drawers... Im is a living man, flesh and blood...

Mr. Williams interrupts this screaming match by roughly ejecting Errol's mother from house.

MR. WILLIAMS: Get out... out... Feel seh yu can come call my daughter anyt'ing cause yu an some gunman friend... See di door yah... Out!

ERROL'S MOTHER: (*Parthian shot*) If you testify, gal, ah pop yu rass!

MR. WILLIAMS: Sharon love, you alright? Lord do, no cry... (*Hugs her*) Hush love, hush. I should neva 'ave let ar in here... Hush, it will all work out...

MUNCHIE: Ah betta be going...

MR. WILLIAMS: Yes. Go.

SHARON: Munchie...

MUNCHIE: Yes, Miss Williams?

SHARON: Come back tomorrow and tell mi what the situation is… Please?

MUNCHIE: Yeah. Later down into di week. Yu res' first. Yu a go need whole heap a strength if yu testify…

SHARON: Dads… what a life eh…? It look like growing up come like good times… Sometimes too much of it and then sometimes none at all… (*Laughs and it turns into crying*) Lord, Dads, I wish ah was still fifteen and living with yu and Ma… Life was so easy then…

MR. WILLIAMS: Yu can always come back home, Sharon; we want yu to come…

SHARON: I know Dads, I know. But I can't, y'know. I don't know but the last few weeks have changed me… I couldn't really be happy there now… That's your life and I want mine…

MR. WILLIAMS: Still, Sharon? After all this?

SHARON: Yeah… I don't know… Yeah, I suppose so…

MR. WILLIAMS: Now Sharon, "suppose so" just isn't good enough. You've put yourself through so much with this silly moving business…

SHARON: Silly, Dads? That's what you call it?

MR. WILLIAMS: Yes, very silly. I'll come for you and all your things tomorrow…

SHARON: No. I am not coming back home… (*Shouting*) I said No… I am not going anywhere. I'm a big woman now. I'm big enough to be raped, so why not to be alone… Do, Dads, just leave me alone…

MR. WILLIAMS: I will not leave you here alone…

SHARON: Yes, you will… (*Gazes meet and a clash of wills is settled*). You will. Because I tell you to. Good night.

MR. WILLIAMS: But Sharon…

SHARON: Good night, Dads.

He hesitates, then leaves.

As he leaves she goes to the door and almost calls him back. Then she goes back to sit in the dimly lit flat, huddled a little.

BENNY'S SONG

This play was commissioned by the Jamaica School of Drama of the then Cultural Training Centre, now the Edna Manley School for the Performing Arts in 1988(?). It was directed as a promenade piece by Earl Warner and the cast was made up of students of the school. The part of Romeo was played by Yrneh Brown.

CAST

BENNY	Late teens
ROMEO	Late teens
MANSON	Late teens
JULIET	Late teens
TIBBY	Early twenties
PARA	Mid twenties
CAPPIE	Early fifties
NURSE	Mid fifties
MISSA J	Sixties
BROTHER LAWRENCE	Fifties
SWEETIE	Late teens
ARLENE	Late teens
POLICEMAN 1	
POLICEMAN 2	
PLAYER 1	
PLAYER 2	
CROWD OF GHETTO DWELLERS	

The play is set in a large open space that changes character as the play demands with the cast creating and dismantling the locations as they are mentioned. The two Players stand and watch over all the action like johncrows perched on a wire looking for carrion.

ACT ONE

Dusk. The players perch like johncrows over the a strip of barren ground, no man's land.

PLAYER 1:   You remember the sound of an Uzi in the night
           And the roar of a nine talking of death
           To children cowering under beds?

PLAYER 2:   Is time to remember and, in the remembering,
           Shed a tear for those who died
           For nothing
           So that even death belched and said,
           Enough, no more.

PLAYER 1:   You give your own too willingly
           And they are too young to have even known
           The sweetness of life
           Their death is a mockery of death
           For they never lived

Sounds of a large and jubilant crowd approaching; they are ringing bells and draped in ribbons and garments of orange. Among the crowd are Juliet, her cousin Tibby and her nurse. The crowd starts to sing the party political anthem "We shall follow Bustamante till we die".

TIBBY: (*Shouting*) Who a go win dis time?

CROWD: We! We!

TIBBY: Who haffi back 'way when Labourite come through?

CROWD: Dem! Mek PNP back 'way!

The crowd grows quieter as they come to cross no man's land. A funeral procession enters from the opposite side. The coffin is draped in green. The procession is led by Brother Lawrence, the undertaker. The two groups come to face each other.

Suddenly a torch flares, then two. The crowd is surrounded with the light in their eyes. Among those confronting the crowd in orange is Romeo, Benny and Manson.

BENNY: Ay, you know where you is, Labourite? A death you come look tonight!

TIBBY: Mouth never kill no-one yet. Back off, man. We no 'fraid a you.

BENNY: You only come like t'ief in the night fi murder people. You no know how fi face dem like man.

TIBBY: You kill one a we, we kill one a you. Dead fi dead.

BENNY: Mi a go finish it den. Di last one you kill was mi mother. One of you going feel it fi she.

MANSON: Jus' cool, Benny, man. Is nuff a dem, you know.

BENNY: Go home, go hide under yu mumma skirt if is 'fraid you 'fraid.

TIBBY: All mi hear is words, mi no see no action. You wasting big people time. Come yah!

The crowd starts to move forward, but Benny draws a knife and goes for Tibby; Tibby grabs a bottle and breaks it. They circle one another in the torchlight. Each side starts to cheer on their fighter as they cut and stab towards each other, funeral forgotten. Romeo pulls Manson aside. Juliet's nurse also pulls her away from the crowd. The undertaker smiles a rueful smile.

ROMEO: This has gone too far now. We have to stop it.

MANSON: Dead fi dead. She was his mother.

ROMEO: But if he dies too, what win but the undertaker?

MANSON: Man haffi do what man haffi do. You suppose to know dat. Labourite fi dead, man. Da's all dem good for.

ROMEO: Benny has too much heart for a fool. He would live longer as a coward.

The fight intensifies as Tibby takes a cut, but it is more shirt than flesh. Benny is fighting as if possessed. A motorbike headlamp blinds the fighters. They freeze. Para walks into the glare of the light. He collars Tibby, sends him to sit on the bike.

TIBBY: Is my fight dis.

PARA: You have to learn how to tek orders, boy. (*To crowd*) Wha' you a stand up yah a look for? Gwon a yu yard! And as fi yu, boy –

BENNY: Is only 'cause you have Para to hide behind, else blood woulda flow tonight, Tibby!

PARA: Mi a go let you live to bury you' mother. After dat, you better walk and watch fi every shadow dat move.

Benny makes to go after Tibby but Romeo and Manson hold him back. Para mounts the bike, stops a moment by Juliet.

PARA: Anybody ever tell you dat you growing real nice? Yu have man yet?

JULIET: Mi no see none worth wanting.

NURSE: Leave the child alone, Para. She too young fi a man like you. You done live and she no start yet.

PARA: Time fi start den.

Nurse puts herself between Juliet and Para. Para kisses his teeth then rides off with Tibby on the back of his bike.

BENNY: Why you stop me?

MANSON: We save you life. You know how much man Para done send off a'ready? Grief a run like madness in yu.

The funeral procession forms up again and goes off. But Benny does not join in. Romeo notices that Benny is not with them and calls Manson. They both go to where Benny is standing alone.

MANSON: Ay, a just 'cause Para come mek you no chop di boy. You see if it was me –

ROMEO: You a go mek dem bury you mother and you no deh to pay you respects? Dat no right, man. You was all she did have.

MANSON: A true, man. Respect due.

ROMEO: I understand how yu feeling but –

BENNY: How him know? How Para know say is fi mi mother? Why him say dat him going to mek mi bury her first?

ROMEO: Time to mourn yu mother, not look to get yuself killed. Lef him to higher dan we in dis business. Our job is just to protect our own.

BENNY: Like Mama? Eeh? Me couldn't protect her, Romeo. Big man like me, wha' me coulda do? Mi in di house a hide while dem have her outside. Mi hear di shot weh kill her, you understand? And is him fire it, Para fire it –

MANSON: (*Sings*) Everywhere is war, mi say war –

ROMEO: You sure a dat, Benny? Yu want me come with you up a di station, mek we tell di police? Dem suppose to be investigating –

BENNY: Mi know is try yu trying to comfort me, mek mi feel say mi no haffi try kill Para myself, but police? Wha' dem good for? Everyday, people dead in dis election; everyday, more and more dead. When dem going to have time fi investigate di murder of a woman who sell sweetie to pickney fi a living?

ROMEO: You don' know for sure say is Para, Benny.

BENNY: You don't know. Mi know. Mi know who kill di old man inna him shop sharing out two dollar rice fi sell? Who kill di youth and tag him, left him in di handcart? Who rape di gal and left her fi dead, mek johncrow pick out her left eye? A war dis, and mi nah hide from it no more. Mama gone. Decency done. A war.

MANSON: Wait, a you dat, Benny? Di man dat always do him school work and stay at him yard? A come you come to join we now?

ROMEO: Benny, listen to me. From school days you were always di one dat know wha' you want to do. You study, turn mechanic, save you money, live good with everybody. Di world and his wife respect you and you mother, how you struggle togedda. If you go kill Para, you is no better dan him.

BENNY: Mi no understand dat. Dat too intellectual fi me. Mi just know weh a go do.

MANSON: You ready fi dead? 'Cause is dat you facing now.

BENNY: Better fi dead so den. From mi a grow, she was di only one show me any kindness, anyt'ing name love. She nah go dead so easy.

ROMEO: Hear wha' den, Benny. You see like how di three a wi is idren from small; mi want you to do somet'ing fi me.

MANSON: You 'memba dem did call us di three musketeers from school days. Especially di gal dem.

BENNY: Play time done, Manson. Is life and death business now.

ROMEO: You listenin' to me? Anytime you decide to mek dat move, you call mi –

MANSON: And mi!

ROMEO: Mek we go with you. You no know the runnings like we. Dis kinda business little fryers like Manson and me usually leave with the generals in di area, but mi understand say dis is somet'ing dat you haffi do. So we will go with you.

BENNY: Is my fight. Mi no want mix you up inna it.

MANSON: A fi wi war. Wi done dead a'ready. You fi promise me, man. Else we nah stop watch you.

BENNY: The three musketeers.

MANSON: Yeah, man. All for one and one for all. How dat poem you write go again, Romeo? Di one you write fi Mandela when dem free him?

Manson starts and they all join in.

ALL: Mi search down the corridor of history
Pass di shadows of slavery and pain
Fi dem few moments of glory
When Black man stand tall again

> Mi tired a di sound of weeping
> And di stink of di slave ships at sea
> Mi looking for a brighter glory
> A time when man mek himself free.

ROMEO: Mi write two more verse for dat one, Manson. Like me did know this was going to happen.

> Benny, if you look back too long
> You' eyes grow weak
> If yu only remember di wrong
> You forget to seek
> The strength inside dat each man possess
> The courage to face tomorrow
> Di wisdom to build a brighter destiny
> Outa di shadows and the sorrow.

BENNY: I hear what you trying to say to mi, Romeo. But is like me heart no want to understand. It too full and if me no ease it, mi a go mad.

MANSON: Mi no tell you say di quiet one dem is di most deadly!

ROMEO: Go and make sure dem bury you' mother right, Benny. She deserve dat from you. And when yu done, come mek we talk 'bout how we going to mek dis move.

Benny leaves.

MANSON: Go after Para? You mad, Romeo? Him kill so much man, him and death is friend, call dem one another by dem first name.

ROMEO: Di guilt a run like madness inna him blood, Manson. Him haffi do something to cool it.

MANSON: But Para? Him no walk nowhere without him irons and 'bout five lieutenant. Him wi shoot you if you look at him funny, a dat me hear.

ROMEO: Sometimes life tek a turn and wi cyan do nutting but follow and see where it tek us.

MANSON: Right now, is reverse gear mi want lick. Dis no feel right. Is di gorgon dem fi settle dis, not we.

ROMEO: All for one and one for all.

MANSON: You as mad as him, to rahtid. You know say mi going where yu going, so mi no know why mi even bother say anyt'ing. Weh you a go do later?

ROMEO: You no think say mi have 'nuff t'ings to t'ink about without walking street and getting myself into trouble?

MANSON: Is di gal you a t'ink bout, all write poem bout her, t'ink me no know. You is di only man mi know dat love woman so. Now dat is your special madness.

ROMEO: When she deh 'bout, is di rest of di world get crazy.

MANSON: You hear how you a talk 'bout her and you no even meet her yet? Is not woman yu love, man. Is love itself.

ROMEO: She will talk to me, man. You no fret 'bout that.

MANSON: Ay, you see when your Rosie walk? Her hips do all di talking to every man in dis place.

ROMEO: Blindness would end dat conversation.

MANSON: Den mi would haffi learn to read with mi fingers. And dat deh is one whole book.

ROMEO: You just looking at the cover. Is a different inside. Sweeter dan you t'ink.

MANSON: Dis man have more serious t'ings fi tink bout. Woman too soft and simple, dem will mek a man weak and sap you' strength like pawpaw tree. Das why mi always tek piece and run. Fi dem weapon deadlier dan any gun.

ROMEO: They cut you inside, where nobody see.

MANSON: Bring you to your knees. Not me, sah. Mi prefer dead. Love haffi wait until war done.

SCENE TWO

A lane in the ghetto. On that lane is the house where Juliet lives with her father and her nurse. Beyond it is an area which is being set up for a dance. During the scene, people are passing, speakers are being set up, vendors are coming in. By the time the scene is over, the dancehall yard at the end of the lane is set up.

PLAYER 1:   But if you think carefully you can recall
Among the debris and the pain
Life, sweet life, struggling in the rain
Of bitterness and gall.

PLAYER 2:   To see each morning break, to draw a breath
Is all there is to remember
Of a time when for all life's harshness
Hope still lived quietly
In the soft light of evening
And shadows in the hall.

PLAYER 1:   But can hope live even in the youngest hands
The coolest dawn
The simplest of plans?

Juliet enters with Tibby, leads him to where she can tend him with bandages brought by her nurse.

JULIET: You lucky. The cut could have been deeper.

TIBBY: It no really hurt.

JULIET: Liar. Why, Tibby? I don't want to go to no more funerals and you are the only cousin I have. Why must you always fight?

TIBBY: Mi no 'fraid of no PNP boy. Is dem start it. Ay, no retreat, no surrender. Is dat Para always say.

108

JULIET: You won't be able to take me to the dance this evening. I won't go then.

NURSE: Which part of you not going? Child, is time you stop read book and start live life. Sixteen is no pickney no more.

TIBBY: You coming, man. Everybody haffi come. 'Cause if Para don't see you deh so, him a go feel say you turn 'gainst we.

NURSE: You no listen to him, you see. Lord, Juliet, you no see how di man dem look after you? Like dem a starve and you is food. God no give woman much power in dis life, and is full time you enjoy likkle of it, before you' waist get wide like mine.

TIBBY: Ay, one likkle scratch can't stop mi, man. And you see how di dance a keep right here anyhow? Me nah miss it. (*Leaving*) And remember you promise to introduce me to you friend. Mi see her a smile at me dis evening and me know wha' dat mean.

NURSE: Dat she no have no sense, dat is weh it mean.

JULIET: Is that all man ever thinks about?

NURSE: It sweet, child. Das why.

JULIET: How would you know? Ever since I can remember, all you have ever done is look after me and papa. If it is so sweet, how come you –

NURSE: Mi bad lucky dat way, child. Man and crosses is di same t'ing to me.

JULIET: So you just lock up shop and decide say no man can sweet you again?

NURSE: Hi! Tek time talk, man. Mind you father hear you. You know him no like when me talk dem t'ings round you.

JULIET: But I know he has his girlfriends.

NURSE: Just because old people don't talk about it, doesn't mean old people don't have feelings.

JULIET: But –

NURSE: Mi just work fi him, child. Mi is not his keeper. Ever since yu mother run gone a 'Merica fi mek life, mi stop talk to him 'bout her or any woman. Mi t'ink dat is the best way.

JULIET: I would never do that, run away and leave my husband, my child. That's why he doesn't even call her name anymore. He hates her.

NURSE: Some t'ings hurt too much fi talk 'bout, child. At least you know who yu puppa is and dat is more dan most. No judge you mother too hard, for she did want to tek you with her, but you father wouldn't let her. You know him is a hard man to please.

Nurse sits Juliet down and starts to unplait her hair for washing.

NURSE: Him love you. In him own way.

JULIET: He would be happier if I was born a boy.

NURSE: Not every love is smiles and kisses, child. But dat no mean it no strong.

JULIET: How do you know when you love somebody? How can you tell?

NURSE: Wait, you skin a ketch fire fi s'mody?

JULIET: It must be wonderful to love somebody so much that nothing else matters.

NURSE: Dat is death, child. Better you love 'till everyt'ing matters.

JULIET: Who did you love?

NURSE: More dan you – who is di daughter mi never did have?

JULIET: I mean real love. When a woman love a man.

NURSE: Di love me have fi you, dat is more real dan all di romance in di world. One day you will know. But mi know how it feel fi yu heart jump when yu see a certain face. Mi know how it feel fi dress and ready and see a man in him zoot suit with di drape shape come fi tek you to Glass Bucket club fi dance till di blood run hot...

JULIET: But did you love him?…

NURSE: Mi did love being young, and mi did love di way di blood rush inna mi veins when me see him, and di hunger in him eyes when him see me. Weh more a young girl want dan dat?

JULIET: Those things don't happen anymore.

NURSE: You no know dat, child.

JULIET: I wish I was a man like Tibby. So I could die young and everybody would come and ban dem belly over me. He knows who he is, I feel like I am still waiting to become.

NURSE: Hush, child. A madness you a chat now.

JULIET: Why? Then Daddy would be proud of me. And you would stop fussing over me. If there is no love then death must be the next best thing. If not, why would so many people die? I don't want to get old and tough like Junie and those girls… Would you cry if I died?

NURSE: Go inside go wash yu hair and stop chat damn foolishness 'bout death. You just start live.

JULIET: This is life?

Juliet goes inside as her father Cappie enters. He walks past the nurse without a word. She stops him.

NURSE: Mi glad you come 'cause mi did want to talk to you bout you daughter's graduation. She no have no frock to wear and mi t'ink dat –

CAPPIE: You cook?

NURSE: Mi no done talk.

CAPPIE: Dem lock down the site today. Sake of di violence. Dem shoot di fore and one of di mason dem.

NURSE: You wi' find work, man.

CAPPIE: Where? You figet a which part wi live? Nobody nah hire a man from di ghetto in dese times.

NURSE: Den don't tell dem weh you live. Now bout di frock –

CAPPIE: A deaf you deaf? Wha' you want me buy it with? Mi blood?

NURSE: Dem cut Tibby today. When we was coming from di meeting. One of di PNP bwoy dem say dat him mother dead.

CAPPIE: Police come? Mi no want no trouble.

NURSE: Police? Fi wha'? Dem no want mix up inna dis. Is Para save him. Why you no talk to Para 'bout work, sah?

CAPPIE: Why yu no look 'bout mi dinner?

A cane tapping and Missa J, a blind man, enters the yard.

NURSE: Is like him have radar. How you say the food done cook, Missa J?

MISSA J: But is you I come to look fah, woman.

CAPPIE: And if you get food, you will tek it.

MISSA J: Manners, man. Just manners.

NURSE: Siddung, Missa J. Mi will serve some fi you and di miserable man here. Mi no know why mi don't go find myself a better job dan work fi dis ungrateful brute.

MISSA J: Which odder man would mek you run him life so?

Nurse goes inside.

CAPPIE: (*sitting with Missa J*) Dem lock down the site. Mi no have no work, Missa J. Mi soon have to walk street and beg like you.

MISSA J: Mi can lend yu mi cane. Mek dem feel sorry fi you.

CAPPIE: Mi would prefer borrow di blindness, so me cyan see what di world a come to.

MISSA J: You woulda still smell it. Talk to me, man. Somet'ing deh pon yu chest. Mi know you too long fi no know dat.

CAPPIE: A dis me come to, Missa J? A dis mi come to, big man like me, a go to a boy, a murderer, like Para fi help? Wha' me good for den? Mi a no man.

MISSA J: A man do weh him haffi do fi mind him family.

CAPPIE: You know why my father mek sure say mi learn a trade? So dat mi never haffi go to no man and beg him anyt'ing. And look now…

MISSA J: If you want good, belly haffi run, Cappie. Suppose you was like me and did haffi depend on people kindness?

CAPPIE: Das why you mauger and look so. No kindness no deh again. You memba when you was di man everyone pack di Carib Theatre fi see of a Christmas morning? Memba when music was music and… Sing somet'ing fi mi, Missa J. Cool off mi soul likkle.

Missa Ja begins to sing and then to move to his mento beat, Cappie watching to make sure he doesn't fall or bump into anything. Tibby, shirt open and combing his hair for the dance, comes out of the house and watches in sardonic amusement.

TIBBY: Ay, is some old time business dat, man. A so man sing nowadays –

Tibby launches into a loud dj version. Cappie backs off, disgusted, but Missa J listens for a while and then starts to put a melody to the rhythm Tibby is riding. Tibby gets more and more enthusiastic until he hurts his injury.

CAPPIE: Next time, no bodda get yuself into any fight den.

TIBBY: And mek dem man do what dem want? Nah, sah. Is war dis, and mi no tek no prisoners.

MISSA J: Yu prefer to end up in General Penitentiary.

Nurse comes out onto the verandah.

NURSE: So wait, di food fi get cold inside waitin' pon yu? You tan deh feel seh me a bring it out to you.

MISSA J: You see why mi haffi love her so?

113

CAPPIE: Better you dan me.

Tibby waits until they are gone inside before he takes a gun out of the waist of his pants. He practices drawing it, posing with it, dry firing it. Juliet, her hair loose after washing, comes out and sees him.

JULIET: I don't have a black dress.

TIBBY: Man can't walk light in dese times.

JULIET: But you are just a boy –

TIBBY: No man nah trouble me and mine.

JULIET: Where did you get it from?

TIBBY: You no mind dat.

JULIET: Para.

TIBBY: Ay, a him rule round yah. Don man. Him like you. You no want turn donnette?

JULIET: I hate how he looks at me. I hate his gold chains. I hate him.

TIBBY: Well, you betta learn fi like him. You father lose him work. You know wha' dat mean. Is Para haffi set him up, and you know say Para like you.

JULIET: Papa would never ask him for a job.

TIBBY: Das why you should do it.

JULIET: Why don't you ask?

TIBBY: 'Cause a no mi him like. A yu. A tell mi how you no mix up with no man and a dat him want: a woman weh no have no more man dan him.

JULIET: You talk about me with him? Like that?

TIBBY: A reality dis, Juliet. (*Going inside*) And one more t'ing. You see my likkle companion yah? (*indicating gun*) Is nobody business but mi own. Yu understand?

JULIET: If yu dead, mi nah go cry.

TIBBY: Mi nah go dead, man. Mi too good looking. Ay, a one way fi get promotion in dis life and mi no intend fi spend my life a box 'bout pon di street. Mi have ambition, Juliet. Nuff ambition.

Tibby walks out to the lane to meet Para's bike and coasts with him to where the dance hall is being set up. People start to arrive for the dance; the music begins to play; men line off eyeing the women; women line off eyeing the men eyeing them. One pair fights briefly and furiously.

Juliet appears on the verandah, watching the goings on. Nurses fusses with her hair, her dress, which is simple, in a light colour, almost virginal. She shrugs off the nurse's hands and sets off towards the dance. Nurse watches her anxiously, then goes inside.

Romeo, Manson and Benny, wearing hat and shades, enter, stand in the shadows.

BENNY: Ay, yu no haffi come with me, yu know. A fi mi fight dis.

ROMEO: We coming, man. We nah go mek you dead so easy. Man cyan walk alone in these times.

MANSON: And a nuff nice gal in yah too. Wha' you say, Benny?

BENNY: A Para mi come for.

MANSON: But if we get a touch offa three nice gal in di mean time, nutting no funny.

ROMEO: You no know what it is like to be in love.

MANSON: Dat a fi brains like you, all dat love business. Me and Benny, we just live it how we find it. You ready?

BENNY: Long time.

ROMEO: If we have to.

BENNY: Wha' you a linger fah? You know seh if dem find out who we is, is death. And a no me a go dead tonight.

Romeo, Benny and Manson approach the dance. Juliet is standing a little way off on her own, looking a little out of place. She catches Benny's eye. She sees him, looks off and then back again. Benny starts towards her but before he can get there, Para goes over to her, leads her to the dance floor. Benny sees him and draws his knife but Romeo and Manson hold him and pull him away.

MANSON: Wha' you did a go do, man? You no see say you woulda dead before you blink?

ROMEO: Wait. Choose the right time. No mek yu heart rule yu head.

BENNY: Him fi dead, man. Dead.

MANSON: Just easy. Time fi dat will come.

The music changes to a slow tune. Para grabs Juliet in close. She pushes him off and runs off. Para is about to go after her when Tibby stops him and goes after Juliet himself. As she passes where Benny is standing, Tibby catches up to her.

TIBBY: You know how much gal would want him?

JULIET: They can have him.

TIBBY: Go back. Apologise to di man.

JULIET: He should apologise to me.

TIBBY: You father want work? Go back, Juliet, before him decide him no want you no more.

JULIET: And what about what I want? What about me? You think he is some kind of hero. But I don't. Leave me alone!

Tibby grabs her hand, is about to take her back to the dance floor when Romeo comes between them.

ROMEO: You no hear di lady seh you are to leave her alone?

TIBBY: Dis is family business.

ROMEO: She free to dance with who she want to dance with.

TIBBY: You deaf?

Manson and Benny come to back Romeo up.

MANSON: No. You?

TIBBY: (*To Juliet*) Pickney days done. You better think hard bout what you doing.

Tibby leaves.

JULIET: Thank you. He didn't mean any harm.

ROMEO: Yeah? You all right?

JULIET: Yes. Thank you.

MANSON: It nah go tek long before Tibby remember who we is. We cyan linger.

JULIET: Don't go.

ROMEO: Outside. Later. Will you be there?

JULIET: Who are you?

ROMEO: Just who you see. Will you wait?

JULIET: Until when?

ROMEO: Cockcrow.

JULIET: By the house by the corner.

Juliet goes back towards dance.

MANSON: You a get confuse, Romeo.

ROMEO: A fi wi war. Nutting to do with her.

MANSON: Come, see Tibby deh a come back.

BENNY: And him a bring backative too. Time to step.

The three leave as Tibby enters with Para, gun drawn and the crowd following. They stream past Juliet after the fleeing boys, as she watches Benny go out of sight.

PLAYER 1: Her heart a beat fast, and she a wonder
If him really going to come

PLAYER 2: Him a wonder if him have di right
To go see if what mek him blood sing
Can find a place in his wounded heart

PLAYER 1:   And in the waiting the heart builds a place
            Where such love can take root and grow

PLAYER 2:   And look up fi find di face of the sun
            No matter which bitter breeze a blow

Outside Juliet's house. The sound of the night all around: dogs barking, distant gunshot, tree frogs. One or two stragglers from the dance walk by, entwined. Romeo waits in the shadows. He looks to the house, up and down the road, returns to the shadows.

Brother Lawrence enters, a large bottle of expensive whiskey in one hand, his undertaker's coat in the other. He staggers a little. Stops to pee into the shadows, so Romeo has to come out.

ROMEO: You should look before you point dat weapon, Brother Lawrence. You never know who you aiming at.

LAWRENCE: What you doing round here, boy? You ready to come visit me a'ready?

ROMEO: I am too young for your business. You have Benny's mother already.

LAWRENCE: Too young? Maybe, maybe. At least you have courage. Join me in a small toast, Romeo.

ROMEO: To who, sir?

LAWRENCE: To politicians, boy, politicians. Without them, where would I be. Business has never been so good. Even if my profits tend to be a little liquid.

ROMEO: (*Watching Lawrence drink deeply*) Does dat make it easier to face di dead, sir?

LAWRENCE: The dead? The dead are my friends, my customers, my boy. No, it is the living I find hard to face. They are afraid of me, you see. To them, I am like God. All men are equal before me. One body is much like the next.

ROMEO: Then why you do it, Brother Lawrence? If you are so lonely. You is a rich man.

LAWRENCE: People need me, boy. You need me. After a miserable life, everyone wants a glorious funeral. Makes it all worthwhile. You sure you don't want a drink?

ROMEO: No. Thank you.

LAWRENCE: Walk with me then. Keep an old man company. I have always liked you, boy. You were different from the rest. Smarter. Kinder. What are you going to do now that you've left school? I could do with an assistant. Come and talk to me about it. Anytime.

ROMEO: I'm waiting for someone.

LAWRENCE: If you wait much longer all you will see is dawn and then dem will see you and you know this is Labourite territory. What is so important that you take this kind of risk, boy? You don't know pattoo flies over this city every night to call more souls home?

ROMEO: Is as important as life, Brother Lawrence.

The door opens and Juliet comes quietly out.

LAWRENCE: I see I am not needed here. But answer me this one, boy, before I go? Why is it that when we have the strength to love passionately, we don't have the sense to love wisely? Take care. These are murderous times.

He staggers off.

Beat

ROMEO: I didn't know if yu were coming again.

JULIET: I had to wait until everybody was asleep.

ROMEO: Soon dawn.

JULIET: Who are you? You were with that boy who wanted to fight Para.

ROMEO: Ask yu heart. You know me just the way I did know you when I saw you.

Beat

ROMEO: Does anyt'ing else really matter?

JULIET: It should.

Beat

JULIET: But it doesn't. Tibby says that you are from across No Man's Land.

ROMEO: Does dat matter?

JULIET: We should be enemies.

Romeo takes her hand.

ROMEO: Soft. Like you eyes. Are your lips soft?

JULIET: Tell me.

They kiss. Juliet breaks away a little.

JULIET: Why couldn't you be one of us?

ROMEO: Or you one a wi. So dat mean you don't love me?

JULIET: Love. You say the word so easy.

ROMEO: And I goin' say it again. Do you love me less 'cause I come from cross No Man's Land?

JULIET: I should. But I can't. Is this love or madness? I don't know. I never felt like this before.

ROMEO: Getting light. I haffi go. When can I see you again? Later? Tomorrow? Tell mi.

JULIET: Where? Not here.

ROMEO: At the funeral home. I'll talk to Brother Lawrence. Dis afternoon. Nobody nah look there. You no 'fraid of di coffins?

JULIET: Not if you are there. Go. Go, before the light betrays you. There are eyes everywhere.

A last kiss and Romeo and Juliet slip away as Para and Tibby come staggering in, loud and full of party.

TIBBY: Yeah, man. We can make that move later tonight, man. Teach dem boys a lesson, a come inna we area like dat.

PARA: An after mi give di boy time to bury him mother before mi kill him too! Wonder if him going to hard to dead same way? Dat old woman fight to di last, man. Respect due.

TIBBY: Dem soon know once and for all who rule round yah.

Tibby turns to go inside.

PARA: Yo, Tibby, remember to tell yu cousin wha' mi say. Mi done play decent now. She turn sixteen and is full time she start tek man. And mi is di best man fi her. Tell her. Say mi choose her, to stop di folly and come come talk to me today. Mi will be pon mi usual corners.

TIBBY: Mi wi' tell her, but –

PARA: You no like di piece mi set you up with, sah? So all mi asking is fi you to set me up di same way.

TIBBY: Still –

PARA: Mi start to wonder 'bout you now, a talk like woman can defy you. Warrior no deal so.

Para wheels off and Tibby watches him go with a worried look on his face. He turns and goes in. Juliet emerges from where she hid and has heard the whole thing.

ACT TWO

PLAYER 1: Now the roar of the guns is fading
           And the gun's flash sparks a new flame

PLAYER 2: And even without knowing why,
           It burns and brightens and quickens
           The beat of life

PLAYER 1: If only for a while
           If only until a louder thunder
           Tells of storms gathering
           Clouds with bellies full
           Of stinging rain.

Juliet is sitting on the verandah steps of her home reading to Missa J who sits on a stool nearby.

JULIET: These happy masks that kiss fair ladies' brows,
           Being black, put us in mind they hide the fair.
           He that is strucken blind cannot forget
           The precious treasure of his eyesight lost:
           Show me a mistress that is passing fair,
           What doth her beauty serve but as a note
           Where I may read who pass'd that passing fair?

Why do you always ask me to read it for you? Do you really understand it?

MISSA J: Memories, child. To hear such old words read by such a young voice. It stirs the memory and soft the sharp edge of reality for me. When you read it, I listen with my heart and I understand. You cyan grudge an old man dat.

JULIET: It's about love, isn't it? Like this one. The one you always ask me to read when you feeling sad.

122

So are you to my thoughts, as food to life,
Or as sweet-seasoned showers are to the ground;
And for the peace of you, I hold such strife
As 'twixt a miser and his wealth is found:
Now proud as an enjoyer, and anon
Doubting the filching age will steal his treasure,
Now counting best to be with you alone,
Then better'd that the world may see my pleasure;
Sometime all full with feasting on your sight,
And by and by clean starved for a look;
Possessing or pursuing no delight,
Save what is had or must from you be took.
Thus do I pine and surfeit day by day
Or gluttoning on all, or all away.

MISSA J: Das di first time you read it like you feeling it, child. You a tun woman pon me.

JULIET: You think that that kind of love can happen now?

MISSA J: Das what mi ponder pon, child.

JULIET: If you think about it so much, how come you are still alone?

MISSA J: You is woman. Juliet, it tek blindness fi teach mi dat looking and loving is not di same ting, and in mi younger days, mi do too much of one and not enough a di odder.

JULIET: Is that what happen to my mother and father?

MISSA J: And a woman hungry fi truth. You father suffer blindness of di heart, child. And in dat darkness all him can hear is him own heart a beat. Love is dere but it get tangle up in di silence, and you mother couldn't tek it no more.

JULIET: I wonder if she thinks about me.

MISSA J: Now is di time mi wish mi had eyes to see you face. Mi hear somet'ing new in yu voice and mi wish mi coulda see it shine inna yu eyes.

JULIET: You see too much a'ready, old man.

Two young women enter, bubbling with laughter: Arlene, who is very pregnant, and Sweetie.

SWEETIE: As if mi coulda want any man like him. Wutless and no ambition, talking 'bout him love me.

ARLENE: A so man stay. Love you till them breed you and den ask you "a who for?". Ay, Missa J, how come you man stay so?

MISSA J: You no hear weh dem a preach dem last days? Just say no.

SWEETIE: Wait, you t'ink me is a permanent virgin like Juliet? Mi cyan say no all di time. A come we come come ask yu wha' really happen to you last night, Juliet.

ARLENE: One minute you a bubble with Para on di dance floor, and di next minute you gone. And Para no dance with any and anyone just so, you know.

JULIET: I had other things to think about.

SWEETIE: Me no did tell you? A fraid she ketch her fraid because she no have no man before.

ARLENE: So a come we come fi gi you instructions, seen? Ay, you see from Para a deal with my friend, mi know say mi safe, so don' bodda run and hide from him next time.

SWEETIE: Mi know you well want hear what we goin' say, Missa J, but dis is fi woman and woman alone.

MISSA J: So wha' you two gal doin' yah, den?

SWEETIE: Is fight you a look? Come, man. Come touch if you bad.

ARLENE: Mind, a dat him well want do.

JULIET: Is all right, Missa J. Is time I learnt the facts of life.

Missa J leaves, tapping away with his cane. Arlene settles herself on the step, leaning back to ease her belly.

ARLENE: Must be a boy. Him start kick out my tripe and him no even born good yet.

JULIET: (*Touching Arlene's stomach*) For good luck. I need it now.

SWEETIE: Serious t'ing now, Juliet. Wha' Para say to you?

JULIET: The usual.

ARLENE: And?

JULIET: And nothing. I don't love him.

SWEETIE: Now you see dat is where all of you young gal tie up yuself, dat is how you get dat belly. You haffi mek sure say love no come inna dis t'ing; from you feel like yu heart start get sof', back off. A worries dat. Jus' mek sure you know wha' you want from him before yu deh with him so when him go outa road pon yu, him get what him want and you get what you want. You understand?

JULIET: And what did you want for that, Arlene?

ARLENE: Dis? At least a dinette set and a double bed. And a crib. And some nice baby clothes –

SWEETIE: And all you get so far is di belly. You gone bad a'ready, man. Is Juliet we come to save.

JULIET: It look like mi gone too far to save now. You too late.

ARLENE: A lie! And all di time wi a swear say you no tek nutting.

SWEETIE: So wha' you a lock up yu mouth for? How it feel?

ARLENE: Like you no know!

SWEETIE: Mi no 'memba di first time.

ARLENE: And mi prefer to forget di first time. Sixty seconds a slipping and sliding and a rahtid beating pon top of it when me reach home.

SWEETIE: So you nah tell wi?

JULIET: Sweet, but it hurt too. Is like you want to do it again, but you fraid.

ARLENE: You know say dat mean we lose di bet. And was di last ten dollar mi did have too.

SWEETIE: So when you going to see him again?

JULIET: He wants to see me today.

ARLENE: Just my luck, eeh? She who nah look man, get two just like dat, and me end up with this.

SWEETIE: Wanty wanty nah getty and getty getty no wanty. So you want to be the new Donnette in the area? Member yu friends when dat happen, you see. Mi woulda look good pon di back of di Ninja bike too, you know.

JULIET: Donnette? I would rather die.

ARLENE: You see her nose start to look any way?

SWEETIE: No, man. Up in the air, same as ever. Just cause you pass CXC and we no reach grade 11 no mean you fi scorn we, you know. Round yah, everybody haffi look out fi everybody else. Especially dem last days.

JULIET: You two don't realise that you are the sisters I never had? That won't change. You should know that.

ARLENE: Something change, though. Something bout you. Mi no know if it good or bad, but you definitely change.

There is the sound of two shots: a man's scream, other shouting and then silence. Sweetie hauls Arlene up from the steps and they both set off energetically to see what the commotion is about.

SWEETIE: You nah come? You no want know who dead?

ARLENE: Mek we go look before police come and start fas' with people.

Nearby lights reveal a man lying face down in the street, shot in the back. A crowd gathers. A man turns him over.

MAN: Is all right. Is not one of we.

WOMAN: Tenk God. Him dead?

MAN: Look so. Three shot him tek. Must dead. You see who kill him?

WOMAN: Even if me did see, me never see. Mi want fi live out mi natural life.

Someone takes a cloth and lays it over the dead man's face.

WOMAN: Young boy too. Somebody waste dem life tryin' to raise him. Waste of time.

The scream of police sirens. Two officers push their way through the crowd which starts to melt away as they arrive. They stand over the body, produce notebooks.

OFFICER 1: Anybody see what happen?

OFFICER 2: Anybody know who him is?

A few kiss their teeth. A woman hawks and spits vigorously near one officer's foot. Soon the officers are alone. Para and Tibby walk up to take a look. Officer 1 drapes Para up by the waist until he stands on tip toe.

OFFICER 1: Wha' you know bout dis, Para?

PARA: Me, sah? Shame, officer. Good boy like me? How me fi know anyt'ing?

OFFICER 2: Might as well just call the morgue.

OFFICER 1: And hope dem come dis time before him start smell up di place. Di last time, dem fling tyre pon a man and burn him, government tink say is a demonstration and start get jumpy. Sarge gi wi hell for bout two weeks.

OFFICER 2: If I never need di gun, me'd a left di job long time. Dem cyan pay man fi do dis work.

They walk away leaving the body where they found it. Two boys come up and start playing marbles nearby. A pedestrian steps over the body on her way. Juliet enters, stands watching for a moment and then drapes the old sheet she has in her arms over the body gently before walking away. Sweetie and Arlene join her.

SWEETIE: You always did have too much heart. Hush. Fi him worries done.

ARLENE: (*Hand on stomach*) Mek wi think bout di living and how we going fi mek sure say dis one no end up so.

They leave together, arm in arm.

In one area, Juliet, Missa J and the nurse, in another, Romeo, Benny and Manson. The scenes happen at the same time as they cross paths but do not meet.

ROMEO: This is different. Different from all di rest.

MANSON: Das what you said last time.

BENNY: So you nah tell wi who she is, man? Mek we go check her out and see if she really cris' enough?

ROMEO: Ay, the sun shining, life is good, everyt'ing is great. Time you figet bout all di worries and mek we start live some life.

MANSON: Mi no tell you you say as soon as you figet bout Rosie, you'd come back to yuself.

BENNY: 'Cause when you in love, you wutless, Romeo. Some worries not so easy to forget still.

MANSON: Ay, mek we go tek in a show dis afternoon. Tek yu mind off t'ings, Benny. What you say, Romeo? The three musketeers ride again?

ROMEO: You gwon. Mi have tings to do.

BENNY: Ay, Manson, mi tink you say Romeo cure of di love business? It look like love still a bite him.

NURSE: And you did promise say you not going to tell no one. Not a living soul, you hear mi?

MISSA J: Who mi fi tell? From yu blind, dem feel seh yu stupid too. But Juliet, you no done tell wi bout di young man yet. Mi like hear you voice when you talk bout him. Like you a sing in church.

NURSE: Stop encourage di girl.

JULIET: It's as if he knows what I'm thinkin' before I think it. And he is so handsome –

NURSE: Mind out fi di handsome one dem, child. A dem bad.

MISSA J: You should know.

NURSE: Hush yu mouth. A fi her man we a talk bout, not mine.

JULIET: I never felt like dat before. When he kissed me –

NURSE: Kiss? Das all?

JULIET: What more you did want us to do?

NURSE: More to di point, if you want to do more, what you need to know. No mek him ruin yu life, child. No matter how him handsome.

JULIET: Ruin it? And it's because of him that I feel alive for the first time.

MISSA J: Now dat is love. Come, missis, you and mi too old fi understand dis. Lef' her to her happiness.

JULIET: You won't tell papa, will you, Missa J?

MISSA J: After him have enough worries a'ready? No, child. Is yu haffi tell him bout dis one.

NURSE: Just wait 'til after him find work, dough. Him miserable enough as it is.

JULIET: But why should he be miserable when I am so happy? Something must be wrong with a world where a father don't want to see his child happy.

NURSE: Das exactly why, child. 'Cause di happiness you feel when yu young no come back again. Him no want you fi turn woman before time. He know dat dat is a heavy burden to bear.

MISSA J: Leave di child alone, woman. No spoil her happiness with yu bitterness.

ROMEO: She has the prettiest eyes. They smile.

MANSON: Mi see odder cheeks whose smile look better to mi.

BENNY: But den, dat is di only cheeks you can see without di paper bag you mek yu gal dem wear.

MANSON: You was watching again?

Romeo takes out a pad and pencil.

MANSON: Time fi step, Benny. Genius at work again.

BENNY: Mek we ketch dat show and lef' lover boy here fi tie himself up with woman. Dem no say actions speak louder dan words?

MANSON: A true, man. Mek we go watch two actor shoot up di place. Mi could do with a rest. Ay Romeo, you know if she have a sister?

Manson and Benny leave.

ROMEO: Through you do know, old friend. Dis love might never find its way into words. The pen would be trespassing on holy ground. Even di tired old sun that was risin' on her face dis morning has burnt her image into me like lightning across a storm sky.

Romeo leaves in the opposite direction.

JULIET: Why is it that time crawls along so slowly? As if every minute was fighting to keep the hand of the clock still. It should pass as quickly as my heart is beating, as fast as my hand is trembling. Is this living? Is this love? It burns me like a greedy, joyful flame and I am happy to give my heart to it… Nurse, I soon come. I going to go see a friend.

NURSE: Mek sure you reach in before dark. Mi no want you outa road any late hours.

MISSA J: But if you come in late, and you no see you nurse, no fret. Mi wi keep her busy.

NURSE: Poor t'ing. Busy with what, please? After yu cyan even see what you a look.

MISSA J: You know dat blind people sense a touch better dan anybody dat can see? Yeah, man. You want me show you?

Juliet slips away while Missa J and Nurse banter. Romeo and Juliet meet at Brother Lawrence's funeral home. In the shadows among the coffins and dried flowers, they find each other, embrace, kiss, kiss again. A voice from the shadows disturbs them.

LAWRENCE: You youngsters no have no respect fi di dead? Di way you a gwon, you would make a dead man rise, so to speak.

ROMEO: We didn't know you were here.

JULIET: We're sorry.

LAWRENCE: I realise that. This old place has been used for many things but this is the first time it has been used for romance.

ROMEO: I thought we could be alone. You said –

LAWRENCE: I said you could meet here. I never said I would let you ruin your lives.

Beat

LAWRENCE: On the other hand, is nice to see some life in this place. You love burn so bright it even mek di shadows dance.

Beat

LAWRENCE: I have to stop drinking so much.

Lawrence leaves.

ROMEO: Your hands trembling.

JULIET: I've never been here before.

ROMEO: Frightened?

JULIET: Not if you're here.

ROMEO: I thought I remembered how beautiful you were. Your skin. But you are even more –

JULIET: After you left, I heard Para talking to my cousin. He wants me. Everyone is pushing me –

ROMEO: And what do you want?

JULIET: I hate him. He likes to be the first. With all the girls in the area. Then he gets rid of them. He wants me now –

ROMEO: What do you want?

JULIET: You.

ROMEO: Tell him you are taken.

JULIET: He will kill you. Unless –

ROMEO: You are taken. Just as I am taken.

JULIET: And if I am taken, he won't want me anymore?

ROMEO: Yes.

Beat

JULIET: There is just us here and now.

ROMEO: And here and now is all there is.

JULIET: Yes. Here and now.

They make love among the coffins then lie in each others arms. Noise from the street outside makes them stir.

Outside the funeral parlour Benny and Manson are coming back from the movie.

BENNY: And you see when him push di nine inna di man mouth and tell him say him mus' beg fi him life? A dat mi want do to di man weh kill my mother.

MANSON: Mek dem bawl living eyewater, man. Is so it fi go. And you see when him drop di guy offa di side of di building after him try stab him, so man fi Rambo.

BENNY: Das what should happen to di likkle one dat run behind Para pee pee cluck cluck. Tibby. Tibby di dibby dibby. Just line him up in my sights and drop him –

Para and Tibby step out of the shadows, guns in hands.

PARA: Is who you calling dibby dibby, bwoy? No you mi see cry like woman over you mother coffin?

MANSON: Just cool, Benny, jus' cool.

TIBBY: Das right, boy. Back off.

Benny runs at Para who grabs him and holds him with the gun to his head. Tibby has his gun on Manson.

TIBBY: Come nuh, since you so bad. Come, man.

MANSON: So you fight, Tibby? You fight against man weh have nutting fi defend demself?

PARA: Weh him was saying, Tibby? Bout push gun inna mout'?

Para pushes the gun into Benny's mouth. Manson moves to go to him; Tibby tries to stop him. Manson and Tibby roll on the ground, the gun between them. The gun goes off. Tibby leaps back in horror as Manson slumps over, clutching his side. Romeo, shirtless, comes out of the funeral home and runs to Manson's side.

TIBBY: Is him try to tek di gun from mi. As God. Mi never mean fi fire it –

PARA: Shut up. Tek up di gun! Tek up di gun, Tibby!

Benny starts to struggle more violently. Para still holds him. Romeo and Tibby go for the gun at the same time. Romeo gets it. He points it at Para.

ROMEO: Let him go. I said let him go.

PARA: Get di rass gun from him, Tibby. Him not going to shoot. Tek di rass gun. Das an order!

Tibby steps forward but Romeo doesn't waver.

ROMEO: I said let him go, Para. It no make sense. Everybody heard di shot. The police soon come. Let him go.

TIBBY: He's right. Come on, Para.

PARA: You is gal, Tibby? Mi say tek di gun from him. Tek di blood claat gun before mi shoot you myself.

Tibby lunges for the gun. Romeo shoots him. He goes down. The sounds of sirens and crowd coming. Romeo sees Para let Benny go as if in a daze. Benny goes over to Manson, turns him over, takes him in his arms. Para escapes through the crowd.

BENNY: You going to be all right. We goin' get you to hospital.

MANSON: I soon be better dan I am now.

BENNY: Where yu hit? Is bad?

MANSON: Mi no feel, mi no feel too bad fi a man das dying.

BENNY: You nah go dead jus' so, man. You forget say is me suppose to dead first?

MANSON: Mi forget, yes. Forgive me, mi friend. But it look like is too late to rememba.

BENNY: No lef wi, Manson. God, wha' yu a punish him fah?

Manson dies. Brother Lawrence and Juliet emerge from the funeral home. She sees Tibby, Romeo with the gun still in his hand, Manson's body.

LAWRENCE: Run, boy. Run before the police reach.

ROMEO: He was coming after me. I didn't mean to kill him. Juliet –

LAWRENCE: Run! Unless you want fi dead yah today too –

ROMEO: I'm sorry. Is death to go, is death if I stay –

JULIET: Why didn't you just kill me too? You have ripped out my heart.

Romeo flees through the crowd as Juliet kneels by Tibby's body. Nobody makes any serious attempt to stop Romeo. Lights down on Juliet kneeling at Tibby's side, Benny cradling Manson's body.

ACT THREE

A graveyard. An open grave waits for a coffin. There is another freshly filled grave nearby.

PLAYER 1:   There was a time when news of a death
                  Meant sadness in the hearts
                  Of those who gathered
                  And smelt the fresh dug earth
                  And the blood-red flowers

PLAYER 2:   But when the election guns cry
                  In the night among the shadows of division
                  Nobody asks why any more
                  Just who. Who is dead?
                  Did I know him? Must I cry again?

Tibby's funeral party approaches the open grave. Juliet and the nurse arrive first. Cappie is not far behind.

JULIET: *(kneeling to touch the earth)* This is such a cold place to lie. Why couldn't we bury him in the sun? He would have liked that.

NURSE: Hush, child. You take dis t'ing too much to heart. You know say man born fi dead.

JULIET: His is a quieter death than mine. I am just as cold as him but the pain doesn't go.

NURSE: Is just di times, child. We living with death too close and it mek all a wi lose heart.

JULIET: Oh, I have a heart. I just don't know where he is.

NURSE: Is time you figet bout him, child. Romeo kill yu cousin and for dat reason, yu fi hate him.

JULIET: I want to hate him. I wish I could.

The coffin approaches, carried by pall bearers, young men including Para. Brother Lawrence is at his theatrical best, walking with the coffin and arranging friends and relatives at the graveside. The coffin is cheap, purple crepe, and flowers on it are common, a little ragged. While they are settling the coffin in place, Brother Lawrence draws Juliet aside.

LAWRENCE: I'm sure I don't need to tell you that yu have my deepest and most heartfelt sympathies.

JULIET: He is the one that is dead. Save your sympathy for him.

LAWRENCE: I have a message for you. From Romeo.

JULIET: Where is he? Is he all right? Tell me!

LAWRENCE: He says he has to see yu. He would risk anyt'ing.

JULIET: So he still loves me?

LAWRENCE: It is more like madness than love, child. He is coming here. He wants you to meet him after the funeral at midnight when everybody gone.

JULIET: This is the right place for us to meet, Brother Lawrence. Here among the graves. That is where his friend is buried. Isn't it funny that this is the only place we can lie side by side without fighting. Here the worms rule.

LAWRENCE: I must get back to the interment. My work is never done, but there is some parts I enjoy more than others. Do you want me to wait with you later?

JULIET: What could I be afraid of now? No. Just go. I'll tell papa I want time to tell Tibby goodbye by myself.

LAWRENCE: Don't stay out too long. I had one girl like you in my parlour and I don't have the heart to prepare another like her. Death is getting old and looking for younger meat to chew on every day.

Brother Lawrence goes back to the gathering around the grave. Sweetie and Arlene come and fetch Juliet. Para comes to stand beside her but Cappie comes to stand between them.

LAWRENCE: His uncle has asked that instead of the usual words, that we should lift our voices instead. Carry this young and restless soul upward with song. I think he would have liked that. Missa J?

The nurse brings Missa J forward and sets him in position. In the quiet he begins to sing "If I had the wings of a dove" and gradually everyone joins in. The coffin is lowered and they step forward one by one to throw dirt on the coffin. The silence and the thudding earth is disturbed by Cappie's voice.

CAPPIE: The night him father dead, him look at mi and say dat him want mi to keep an eye on him son, Tibby, his one son. And dat is what me do, all dese years, all dis time.

Mi watch him grow into a man, watch him learn how fi live in dis world, and mi try mi poor best fi mek sure dat him no do without.

Fi wha'? Fi wha'? Fi come stand at him graveside, fi see not even one grey hair, not one wrinkle, nothing fi tell yu say him live likkle life. Better him dead with him father, better him never born dat fi dead so. Him was di only son mi ever know, and when di spirit of anger bun in him, mi woulda tell him fi sekkle off, tek it easy. But mi know how him feel. Now mi know dat him never stand a chance from di day him born. Him mighta dead but at least him gone outa dis world dat no give no poor man a chance fi nutting more dan death.

Juliet tries to lead him away, but he brushes her off. The others start to leave, drifting away in uncertain ones and twos. Just Juliet, Cappie and the nurse are left. Para hovers nearby. Brother Lawrence goes over to Cappie and leads him away with the nurse's help. They are stopped by Para.

PARA: Mi sorry dis happen. Him was a good boy.

NURSE: We no want hear nutting from you. Is you lead him inna bad company.

PARA: You no understand nutting. A man haffi do what a man haffi do.

NURSE: What kinda man give a boy like dat a gun?

PARA: Who you a chat to?

LAWRENCE: She no mean it, Para. Is di grief talking.

NURSE: No tek di truth from mi, Bredda Lawrence. Is all mi have left.

PARA: Is Cappie mi come to talk to. Mi and him have some business to finish.

NURSE: You no done suck di family blood yet, parasite?

The nurse gets Juliet and leaves reluctantly with Brother Lawrence.

PARA: Before him dead, Tibby tell me you a look work.

CAPPIE: Mi wi find work. Mi no need no help.

PARA: Tek it fi Tibby. Dem have a site soon open on Charles Street and is mi control it. Go go talk to the fore.

CAPPIE: Dis funeral cost everyting mi have. And mi still never do wha' mi did want fi him.

PARA: Him wi understand. Him always was a sensible yout'. Understand say yu cyan get something fi nutting in dis life.

CAPPIE: At least now mi can send Juliet to go register at di college. At least she can have someting better in dis life.

PARA: A dat me a tell Tibby. Dat she deserve something better. Keep herself so nice and sweet, no mix up with no man.

CAPPIE: She taking Tibby death hard. She sit for hours. Alone. As if she has lost her heart.

PARA: Ay, you tell her say me a go come fi her dis evening. Tek her out, mek her enjoy herself likkle. It no right fi somebody so sweet mourn fi too long.

CAPPIE: Mi wi ask her if she want to go.

PARA: No, man. You going tell her. Just like how mi tell di fore say you going to work at di site. You understand me? Mi know wha' good fi her, man. You just do wha' mi say.

CAPPIE: But –

PARA: Tibby did say dat you was a stubborn man. Ay, yu better friend me up now, 'cause after we win di election, who you t'ink a go rule round yah? (*Laughs*)

Para leaves the cemetery followed slowly by Cappie.

Later that night in the cemetery. Juliet enters with her nurse.

NURSE: Dis is madness, child. Mi cyan' lef you here. Too many dead ones weh no pass over yet.

JULIET: Please. You have to leave me alone. Or he won't come.

NURSE: You no 'fraid of duppy, child? You no 'fraid something happen to you?

JULIET: Tibby is dead. Romeo is gone. I have cried until I have no more tears left. What could be worse than that? Why should I be afraid of ghosts? It would be more like a reunion, so many of my friends are dead.

NURSE: But dis is not love, child. Dis is folly.

JULIET: This makes more sense to me. Go. Leave me alone.

NURSE: You come and you see him is not here. Come back to the house with me. Him will try get in touch with you again.

JULIET: No. You don't understand. This I where I feel most at peace. I'm not afraid. At least here I have some hope for happiness. Don't ask me to go.

NURSE: I waiting for you den. Out by di road. If mi no see you come out, mi coming back fi you.

JULIET: (*Kisses her*) You can't look after me all my life. Didn't you say that I was a big woman now?

139

NURSE: And mi wish mi bite out mi tongue now. Words without thought is the most dangerous of weapons.

The nurse leaves reluctantly and Juliet goes to sit among the gravestones. She curls up, hums to herself. Looks up as a megaphone on a car passes blaring "Everyone has a vote, everyone has the right to decide who will lead this country. Dip your finger in the ink tomorrow for progress, for freedom. Poor people time now. Time fi mek a change". There is the distant sounds of a crowd singing party songs.

A movement in the shadows and Juliet gets up expectantly. Para enters. She tries to walk past him, but he grabs her arm.

PARA: Is wha' kinda kinky message dat you send to mi? Mi no like no woman weh play games, you know.

JULIET: I never sent you any message.

PARA: You no hear me say mi no want no romping? Done di game. You no need to pretend no more, cause mi come. Yu man is here.

JULIET: He isn't here.

PARA: Mi haffi admire how your father work, sah. Him no waste no time. But hear me now, dis cemetery business cyan work. You to figet bout all dis death business.

JULIET: How can I, when you smell of it.

PARA: Who you a chat to, gal?

JULIET: What does my father have to do with all this?

PARA: You no fret bout dat. You just do wha' him tell you. Dat is between big man. Come, man. You no need to frighten. Mi know say is yu first. Just relax and enjoy it. A dat me always tell my woman dem.

JULIET: Did Papa tell you that I was a virgin too? He lied, Para. He sold you damaged goods.

PARA: Just easy, man. You no haffi fight me so.

Juliet stops struggling and instead starts to move towards him.

JULIET: Fight? I don't want to fight. I want to feel like that again, to have a man's body next to mine, feel how he wants me –

Juliet goes to touch his crotch and he jumps back, brushing her off.

PARA: Is wha' you a do, man? A gwon like any old whore.

JULIET: (*Laughs*) If my father sold me to you, isn't that what I am? (*Advances on him*) Well? Don't you love me any more, Para? Can't you compete with the lover I've had? Why don't you use your gun instead? After all, that is your manhood, isn't it, Para?

Para goes to draw his gun but Benny and several other youths emerge from the shadows, hold him and take the gun from him.

BENNY: Just relax and enjoy it, man. A no dat you did say?

JULIET: You sent the message with Father Lawrence. You were at the dance with Romeo. Where is he?

BENNY: Go home, gal.

JULIET: Does he know I'm waiting?

BENNY: Mi no have no quarrel with you. Run. And if you tell anybody weh you see yah tonight, you a go dead next.

JULIET: Where is he? Isn't he coming?

BENNY: Mi say run, gal!

Juliet moves away but doesn't go far.

PARA: Is wha' mi do you, man? Wha' you a hold me fah?

BENNY: You no know mi, Para? Look pon mi good. You no memba how you give mi time to bury mi mother? Eeh? Well, see her grave deh. You want see it.

PARA: She wasn't suppose to dead, man. She did in di wrong place, das all. Mi no kill woman.

BENNY: Di whole of you is murderer. You no see say is mi friend grave you a stand side of? You memba him? Di one weh Tibby kill? Even when him is dead, him is friend to me and enemy to you.

At Benny's signal, one of the men digs in Manson's grave and produces a cloth bundle and unwraps a gun.

BENNY: When dem find you a morning, dem a go find you with a bullet inna yu head and yu gun inna yu hand, di gun weh kill so much people –

PARA: A politics, man. Is nutting personal. You suppose to understand dat. Is no mi decide to do it. Is tell dem tell mi to do it. Is orders mi get.

BENNY: Dem? Dem who? Mi no see none a dem here inna di dirt and stink. Mi no see none a dem a come to di funeral dem, mi no see none a dem lose dem friend, dem family, dem life every day.

PARA: But you know how it go, man. If man and man going to mek life, dem haffi find dem way in di politricks, dem haffi find a one to work fah. Is so poor people survive.

BENNY: Work? Is work you call it fi walk street at night like vampire and kick off people door, a kill pickney and woman weh a breed?

PARA: From you have something, everybody want tek it from you. Yu haffi defend yuself. Else dem a go say dat you sof'.

BENNY: So dead like a big man den nuh? Wha' yu a tremble so fah?

PARA: Mi one cyan change it. Is so dis country go from mi was a boy. Whoever win, di rest a go suffer.

BENNY: Well, mi study it good too and yu know what, mi feel say you right. And since mi and you come from different areas, since me a PNP and you a Labourite, guess what? Is dead you a go dead tonight.

PARA: Dem wi come after you. Dem nah go rest until you dead too.

BENNY: When yu dead, dem jus' a go find somebody else to terrorise poor people. Dem not even going to piss pon yu grave. Ay, mi no want talk no more.

Benny pushes the gun in Para's mouth. Juliet screams. The other youths drag her out of the shadows.

BENNY: Mi no tell yu fi run, gal? Mind mi haffi kill yu in yah tonight. Dis is one a fi yu own, Para? Eeh? Yu want fi see her tek some real man before she dead?

PARA: Yeah, man. Yu gwon, man. She young and fresh. She no tek man yet.

BENNY: And yu gi' her away so easy?

PARA: Is just woman. Wha' yu expect?

BENNY: Like mi modda was just woman. Now mi understand you better and better. You know how fi pray?

JULIET: Don't. Don't kill him.

BENNY: You a beg fi yu man, gal?

JULIET: I am begging you. You hate him for killing but you are going to do the same thing. Then you will die. The cycle never ends. You already have his gun.

BENNY: You come come play righteous with me? Eeh? Dis is di house of di dead, gal. Nutting no mean nutting here more dan death itself. Wha' you say? We coulda shoot you with Para gun, den kill him. Easy.

JULIET: Can't you see I am half dead already? This, this is my cousin's grave. And tonight I was to meet Romeo here but it looks as if even that –

BENNY: You? You is di gal dat get inna him head?

JULIET: If it wasn't for your hatred, your vengeance, he would still be here. I have a right to hate you too. All of you. And all I feel is sadness. Such bitter, deep sadness.

BENNY: Is wha' do you, gal? You a get off.

JULIET: So it is madness to love. That is what you and your guns and your corpses calls madness.

Juliet goes to stand in front of Para.

JULIET: Don't do it. It is punishment enough to be what he is.

BENNY: Could never be enough.

Benny slaps Juliet and she falls, hitting her head on the gravestone.

BENNY: Time fi dead now, Para. Nobody a go win dis election tonight.

Benny raises the gun to fire. Hesitates. Firms himself and raises it again. Romeo steps into the light. He is out of breath from running. The sound of voices chasing him, the light of bottle torches in the distance.

BENNY: Wha' you a do yah?

ROMEO: I had to come. To see her. Dem sight me.

BENNY: Gwon. Run. Mi wi stop dem.

Romeo sees Juliet looking lifeless.

ROMEO: I have nowhere to go now. I was coming here to my life.

Tries to rouse her and cannot.

ROMEO: But she is gone.

BENNY: Is wha' do you, man? You no hear mi say you fi run?

ROMEO: Where? There is nowhere left to go.

Romeo takes Juliet's body in his arms.

ROMEO: Nothing left to live for.

Romeo gently rocks her body.
Para breaks away from his captors, running towards the torches. Benny's friends start to leave in the opposite direction.

PARA: Over yah so! Di bwoy over yah!

BENNY: Come! Lef' di gal. Dem a go kill you!

ROMEO: Her skin was so soft. Soft.

Benny tries to drag Romeo away but Romeo fights him off and goes back

144

to Juliet. Benny hesitates and then he and the last of his friends depart as the crowd enters. The nurse follows them in.

PARA: See him yah! See di murderer yah! Is try mi did try stop him from hurting her. Hold him!

NURSE: Mi know dis would bring more sorrow. Mi poor sweet child, mi little dove –

She kneels by Juliet as the crowd drags Romeo off. They start to beat him, hopping and jumping like johncrows. He doesn't fight back, goes down willingly. The nurse tries to wake Juliet as the frenzy of killing dies down. The crowd draws back to show Romeo's body on the ground. Juliet comes slowly round and sees it. She crawls over to it and puts her head on his broken chest.

PARA: Ay, tek her off him, man. Pick her up.

A man comes forward to help her. She grabs the knife the man has in his waist and turns to face the crowd.

JULIET: You sure you had enough? You sure his sweet blood on the ground is all you want? Look at him. Have you hurt him enough? Have you punished him for loving me?

NURSE: Hush, child. No talk so. Come, mek we go home.

JULIET: I am home. He wanted us to be together. And I want whatever he wants. There is nowhere else to go.

Juliet stabs herself. Falls.

NURSE: Stay with mi, child. No love sweet enough to die for.

JULIET: It is better than this life. (*Touches Nurse's face briefly*) Though there are a few people I shall miss.

Cappie makes his way to where she lies. There are calls of "Call di ambulance" from someone in the crowd. Missa J follows Cappie, making his way through the crowd that stands in uneasy silence.

MISSA J: What happen? Who dead? I never yet hear such a terrible silence.

CAPPIE: (*Bellows his pain*) Juliet!

JULIET: Did you have to sell me for so little, Papa?

NURSE: You a mourn you son so much, you mek you daughter slip through yu hands. No touch her, man. Is too late for left over kindness.

CAPPIE: Mi child. Mi one sweet child.

Juliet dies.

PARA: She tek up with bad company. Wha' she doing inna cemetery dem hours a night? Dem nowadays young gal too bad.

Cappie goes after Para but Missa J comes between them.

MISSA J: For all yu sight, you no see it yet, old friend? For all yu sense, yu no understand nutting? Yu child dead before she even tun woman good and all yu can tink bout is death? And di whole a you, standing round di place like a flock a johncrow, wha' more you need to happen before you understand?

Look, look and tell mi. Don't di two a dem blood red same way? Look again and tell me. Don't dem is young same way? If dem was born in a different time, in a different place, among people who no figet how to love and live, dese two young people would mek all a we proud. But look wha' happen now. Look wha' bring dem down in di dirt now, fi dead like any mongrel dog a roadside. Dem did dare fi love dem one anodder, dem did dare fi try love when everybody a teach dem fi hate, try gentleness when dem no know nutting but violence and hatred.

You know who responsible fi dem death? You know who? You! Di whole a you stand up deh and a look pon dem. You! Because you mek hatred rule you, you mek greed and vanity and spite run yu life. You poor and yu life hard and yu feel somebody fi blame fi dat. Somebody come yah and stand pon a platform and buy you curry goat and smile with you and tell you say yu problems come from dem over dere. And you tek you damn foolish selves and follow dem. Eat di goat and dance to di music and lose you self respect.

Where dem is now? Dem is not here in dis graveyard. Dem is in dem house safe and sound, a plan wha' dem going to do when you vote fi dem. Plan how dem going to persuade you to mek you dead Uncle John and crazy Aunty Gee vote fi dem too. Lie and cheat and steal fi dem. And now dem going pinch piece offa di corner of wha' dem have to fling to you, mek you fight like puss and dog over it, mek you kill one anodder over it, mek yu disrespect yuself over it.

PARA: Ay, old man. No one no want to hear wha' you haffi say.

NURSE: Mek him talk. Is you blind.

MISSA J: Yu know when di killing a go stop? You know when you going to be free? When yu decide say no one, no politrickster, no gunman, no drug dealer, nobody going to tell you what to do. Cause you know. All of you know. Figet di vengeance. Figet di hatred. Look pon dem two poor young people. No mek dis happen for nutting. Memba everybody you know, everybody you care bout dat die through violence, and use dat memory to make you strong. If you do dat, tomorrow no matter which party have power, a we win. If you no do dat, yu blind more dan me. If dis no teach we say we haffi love di way dese two young people did love, den when we ever going to learn, lord? When we ever going to learn?

Missa J loosens a neckerchief he wears around his neck and reaches for the nurse.

MISSA J: Woman, tek mi to put dis pon di grave dem. Mi want all of yu fi see it when you pass.

Missa J lays the neckerchief on the grave.

MISSA J: Dis fi di boy that dead fi love in a world where love have no place.

NURSE: (*unpinning a brooch*) And dis for di sweet child dat would not learn the lesson of hate and love hope more than life.

LAWRENCE: (*He lays down his undertaker's hat*) This for the courage to try, and death's defeat in that victory.

There is a disturbance at the edge of the crowd. Benny, gun in hand pushes his way through to the graveside. There is a waiting silence.

MISSA J: Who dat a bring di smell of death back inna di place? Wi tired of it now.

BENNY: Not you one, old man. Not you one.

Benny goes forward and kneels beside Romeo. He straightens his body, closes his eyes. He goes over to his mother's grave and puts his gun down on it.

BENNY: (*quoting*)
Di wisdom to create a brighter tomorrow
Out of the shadows and the sorrow.

You keep that for mi, Mama. Mi no want fight no more. It tek mi a long time to understand what you always used to say to mi, but now mi see it clear. Death is too easy and life is di struggle. Me nah run way from it no more.

One by one members of the crowd come forward and put their mementos onto the pile. They lift the bodies up and carry them off. Missa J begins to sing a hymn and the rest join in until the sound is full and rich, rising to the skies.

THE END

THE KEY GAME

This play was commissioned and produced by Talawa Theatre Company and directed by Karena Johnson. It ran at Riverside Studios in London from October 3rd to 19th 2002. The cast consisted of Jim Findlay as Norman, Kevin Harvey as Shakespeare, Sylvano Clarke as Dappo and Marc Matthews as Gonzales. The production won four star reviews and was chosen as *Time Out* magazine's pick of the week.

CAST

NORMAN   A nurse. Mid forties

GONZALES   A thin, wiry man in his sixties

SHAKESPEARE   A long, thin man in his forties

DAPPO   A sturdy young man in his twenties

SET

The stage is set as a ward in a dilapidated Victorian asylum in the Caribbean. There are three beds, a small desk and a locked cupboard. The windows are set high in the walls, recessed into arched alcoves and are barred but with no glass. The sea and a few thin palm trees can be seen in the distance beyond the windows.

There are three beds, occupied by the patients. A desk, chair and a locked cupboard make up the rest of the set. The main entrance to the ward is a sturdy double door, with a large keyhole.

ACT ONE

The late 1990s

The play begins at dawn. As the light comes up, Gonzales gets out of his bed, climbs on the desk and from there into one of the window alcoves where he perches staring out at the sea. He is medicated and moves slowly, concentrating hard on what he is doing.

GONZALES: Land breeze blowing. Blow you out to sea sweet as sugar.

Dappo turns over in bed, covering his ears, trying to get back to sleep.

GONZALES: Sun bouncing off the sea. Cause sea blindness if you not careful.

Shakespeare moves in his bed, then sits up abruptly, looking around him in panic. Sees where he is and calms down.

SHAKESPEARE: Would it be too much to ask for you to maintain some semblance of silence at this ungodly hour of the morning?

He gets out of bed and begins to straighten it. He strokes it five times at each corner then walks around it twice before he sits on it and gets up twice.

Dappo sits up and glares at Shakespeare. Gonzales ignores them both.

A bolt is drawn on the outside of the door. Then the key goes into the door. Dappo gets out of bed.

SHAKESPEARE: About time.

The door opens, revealing the words Ward 11 painted on the outside, and Norman enters, a large, ebullient man. He is dressed in a nurse's uniform that is a little grubby.

NORMAN: Morning, gentlemen. Morning.

He closes the door and hangs the large key from the front door on his belt. He crosses to where Gonzales is perched and helps him down as he has done many times before.

NORMAN: Old man like you. You going break your neck one of these days.

Gonzales goes back to sit on his bed. He takes three or four large, turquoise-coloured pebbles out of his pocket and sits, staring at them.

NORMAN: (*Sniffing*) Somebody smelling a little high today, man.

Dappo moves away backwards from Norman, twisting and turning so that he doesn't face either of the other two.

NORMAN: Not you today, Dappo. No philosophy this morning, Shakespeare?

SHAKESPEARE: Pearl before swine. A word to the wise is sufficient.

DAPPO: You need a bath.

SHAKESPEARE: Grooming is important. Women notice that.

DAPPO: I like fucking women. I'm the best fucker. I told the Prime Minister.

GONZALES: Fucking women.

NORMAN: Too early for that argument, gentlemen.

Norman unlocks the cupboard. Dappo walks around him, trying to see what is in there. Norman blocks his view. He takes out soap, a rag and a ratty towel.

NORMAN: Come on, Shakespeare. Time wasting.

SHAKESPEARE: Coming.

He sits on the bed and gets up three times, puts on then takes off his

154

slippers and straightens them at the side of the bed, He does that five times.

DAPPO: Fucking idiot.

Shakespeare looks up and loses count. He starts again, to Norman's impatience. Dappo laughs.

GONZALES: Sea blindness.

Norman waits patiently until Shakespeare is finished.

NORMAN: Remember, Shakespeare. Just soap up and rinse off. No lingering today.

They leave the ward together, Norman locking the door behind him. Dappo begins his routine of morning exercise, mumbling to himself about his mission as he does so. Gonzales begins to rock as he rolls the pebbles around in his hands. One of the pebbles slips from his hand and bounces across the ward. He gets up to go and look for it.

DAPPO: You think I don't see you? You think I don't see you? Making manoeuvres against me all the time. Creeping around.

Gonzales continues to look for his pebble.

DAPPO: Any day now. Any day now. I not staying here forever. I need to speak to the Prime Minister about this.

Gonzales finds his pebble. He brushes it off carefully. Dappo backs closer to him.

DAPPO: Is a worldwide conspiracy. But my mission is too important. Nothing is going to stand in my way, you get me?

Gonzales moves to go back up into his perch by the window. Dappo blocks him. Gonzales tries to go around him. Dappo blocks him again. Gonzales tries to climb on the cupboard to get away from him. Dappo, suddenly angry, grabs him and pulls him down, scattering his pebbles.

DAPPO: I trying to tell you something. You just don't want to understand. Is for your own good. I am the only one who can lead you out of the valley of death.

Gonzales suddenly begins to fight furiously against Dappo and pushes him off, diving for his pebbles, scrabbling to recover them. Dappo is winded.

DAPPO: You know who you defying? You want to die?

Dappo begins to exercise vigorously, glaring at Gonzales as he does so.

DAPPO: You ready to die, old man?

GONZALES: Any time. Any time now.

Gonzales climbs to the window perch again, looks out, rocks himself.

DAPPO: Fucking idiot.

Dappo puts his hands over his ears.

DAPPO: (*To the voices in his head*) I doing my best! What more you want me to do? I am not responsible for him. Every man for himself.

Dappo goes back to exercising.

GONZALES: (*Sings repeatedly*)
    Brown skin gal, stay home and mind baby,
    Brown skin gal, stay home and mind baby.
    I going away, on a sailing ship
    So if I don't come back, stay home and mind baby.

Dappo tries to keep focused on his exercise, but the singing eventually eats into his concentration and he has to stop.

DAPPO: Too much noise. Quiet! Quiet!! You trying to mad me?

Norman and Shakespeare re-enter. Shakespeare taps the door frame several times before he will come through. Norman goes over and takes Gonzales down from this window perch.

NORMAN: I leave you men here for five minutes and this is what I come back to find? Shame on you.

Gonzales ignores him, going over to his bed. Dappo flexes his muscles at no-one in particular.

NORMAN: Right. Medication then breakfast.

DAPPO: He attacked me. While you were gone. What you going to do about that?

SHAKESPEARE: Do I need this? No manners, no brought upsy, nothing.

Shakespeare tries to go to his bed, Dappo backs across his path. Shakespeare has to go back to the door and begin his ritual of entering again. He knocks again then sets off for his bed. Dappo makes to block him again, but Shakespeare slips in behind him so that he can't see him and so gets back to his bed.

NORMAN: We all struggling along together on this ward for so long, you don't think is time you all learn to live good with one another?

Norman goes to the cupboard and unlocks a box with medication. It is just about empty. He tries to hide this from the patients. He sets out the medication with some water.

DAPPO: Pen and paper. I need fucking pen and paper.

SHAKESPEARE: Why? You wouldn't know what to do with it.

DAPPO: (*To voices*) Eeh? Spare him? Why? I could kill him. I could.

Shakespeare takes a book out from under his mattress. He opens it and finds page fifteen then closes it. He repeats the action. Dappo comes over and grabs the book.

DAPPO: Pen and paper!

Norman wearily goes and restrains Dappo who doesn't put up much of a fight. Shakespeare reclaims his book and begins his opening ritual again. Norman lets Dappo go and tries again.

NORMAN: Today is a bad day and I'm in no mood for foolishness, gentlemen. Time for medication.

SHAKESPEARE: You wife give you a hard time this morning? You don't treat her well. She wouldn't give you a bad time if you treated her well.

DAPPO: You have a wife? Eeh? You have a wife? You know anything about wife, Shakespeare?

Shakespeare is distressed and begins rubbing his hands over and over again. Norman gives Gonzales his tablets first.

NORMAN: Enough, Dappo.

Gonzales, seeing that he is preoccupied, slips his medication down his trousers then tries to climb back up to his window perch again.

NORMAN: Things are going to have to change around here.

SHAKESPEARE: What kind of change?

DAPPO: About time. My time has come.

NORMAN: Medication first.

Norman gives Shakespeare his medication.

SHAKESPEARE: Just one today?

NORMAN: Take it, Shakespeare. Dappo?

DAPPO: I feel fine. I feel good. I'm healthy.

NORMAN: Because you are taking your medication.

DAPPO: I don't need medication. That lithium is poison. They warn me all the time.

Dappo takes his pills.

SHAKESPEARE: Chemical oblivion. Imitating the sweet sleep of Lethe, the soft touch of death. (*Quotes*) My heart aches, and a drowsy numbness pains/My sense, as though of hemlock I had drunk/ or emptied some dull opiate to the drains...

The other patients have heard all this before and pay him no mind. Shakespeare gives up in disgust, returning to sit on his bed.

Norman goes over to Gonzales and holds out his hand. Gonzales digs the tablets out of his trousers and goes to hand them to Norman.

NORMAN: Just take them, old man.

Gonzales takes them.

NORMAN: News from above. Pay attention. This affects all three of you.

Dappo goes to sulk in the corner, Shakespeare keeps stroking the bedclothes smooth, Gonzales gets out his pebbles again.

NORMAN: You been here so long, they can't find your files in administration. Nobody's fault. An administrative oversight. They've asked me to get your details. Dappo, start with you. Dappo?

DAPPO: Confidential. Top Secret. My mission is not yet over.

NORMAN: Name?

DAPPO: Name, rank and serial number. 1, 2, 3, 4, 5, 6, 7, 8, 9.

NORMAN: Hearing the voices again, Dappo?

DAPPO: What voices? Who said anything about voices?

NORMAN: Your real name, Dappo. I need it for the records.

SHAKESPEARE: David.

DAPPO: Isn't.

SHAKESPEARE: You said it was. I remember.

DAPPO: To fool you. Isn't David.

NORMAN: (*Writing*) David. David what, Dappo?

DAPPO: They beat prisoners. They want them to confess. Name, rank and serial number. 1, 2, 3, 4, 5…

SHAKESPEARE: Marchand.

DAPPO: I never confessed. Tortured me, kept me awake all night, beat me with a tamarind switch, starved me until I had to thief what was left in the pot bottom at night. I never confessed. I had my mission.

SHAKESPEARE: He used to live with his grandmother some-where up in the hills.

DAPPO: Herne Hill.

NORMAN: (*Writing*) David Marchand, Herne Hill. Which parish?

DAPPO: London. Herne Hill, London.

NORMAN: I need to know where you lived before you came here.

DAPPO: Brought me here. They gave her a packet of Milo and a tin of condense milk as a reward. Brought me here in chains but I didn't confess.

NORMAN: Who brought you in, Dappo?

DAPPO: Name, Rank and serial number. 1, 2, 3, 4, 5, 6, 7, 8, 9.

NORMAN: All right, my son. Just calm yourself. Nobody trying to hurt you here.

DAPPO: 1, 2, 3, 4, 5, 6, 7, 8, 9!

Dappo begins to flex his muscles aggressively at Norman who knows the best thing to do is ignore him.

NORMAN: What about you, Shakespeare?

SHAKESPEARE: Gilbert Aloysius MacFarlane. 56 Harbour Street. Aloysius spelt A L O Y S I U S. You have that?

NORMAN: I think so. How long have you been here, Gilbert?

SHAKESPEARE: Nobody calls me that.

NORMAN: Shakespeare then. How long?

SHAKESPEARE: I forget.

NORMAN: Ten years? Fifteen years?

SHAKESPEARE: Nice old house on Harbour Street. Big mango tree shaded the front verandah. Very genteel.

NORMAN: Nobody lives on Harbour Street any more, Shakespeare. It's all businesses, offices, restaurants. Has been for twenty years. You been here that long?

SHAKESPEARE: I forget.

Shakespeare is getting anxious and begins to rub his hands. Then he goes back to his bed and begins his ritual of sitting and standing.

NORMAN: Think about it and tell me when you remember something then. What about you, old man?

GONZALES: I have no home to go to. It burnt down.

NORMAN: No friends? No family?

GONZALES: No.

NORMAN: Come on, gentlemen. Don't any of you remember anything useful about life outside of this place?

GONZALES: Gonzales. Gonzales. Raymond Gonzales.

Gonzales walks away.

NORMAN: Try to understand. They need this information for the files. All completely routine.

All three patients have by now become distressed, withdrawn. Dappo is pacing and talking to himself vigorously. Shakespeare is sitting and standing, opening and closing the book, Gonzales climbs to his window and will not come down.

A loud banging on the ward door. A shout of "breakfast!" Norman takes the key off his belt and opens the ward door. A tray with a sliced loaf of hard dough bread and an urn of tea are outside. He brings them in. Then locks the door and hangs the key back on his belt. He opens up the food in silence. Dappo and Shakespeare watch him, their distress lessening. Gonzales ignores it all.

NORMAN: Once you get a little food in you belly, you will feel right as rain. Trust me. Dappo? Three slices of bread? A man on a mission has to eat to stay fit.

Norman gives Dappo his bread and a cup of tea. He crosses to Shakespeare.

NORMAN: Come on, Gilbert. Woman don't like a mauger man.

161

SHAKESPEARE: I, Gilbert Aloysius MacFarlane, take thee…

DAPPO: Take thee, mattress, to be my wedded wife… You think I don't see you fucking the mattress at night? Eeh?

Shakespeare rearranges his slippers.

SHAKESPEARE: Spelt A L O Y…

NORMAN: Don't pay him any mind, Shakespeare. Besides, you can't get married before breakfast. Come and eat.

Shakespeare comes reluctantly to take the bread. He nibbles at each of the sides equally, stopping to make sure that the slice remains symmetrical.

DAPPO: Tea is fucking cold. Can't ease the gas from my stomach if it is cold.

NORMAN: Just one slice today, Gonzales.

Gonzales shakes his head.

NORMAN: You want the tube again? You know I can't let you starve yourself.

GONZALES: The tube.

NORMAN: You know is not something I like to do, G.

Gonzales hesitates, as if he is going to come down, but then turns his back on him. Norman contains his slight irritation and climbs on his chair to get up to his perch.

NORMAN: One slice. For me.

Gonzales takes the slice of bread. Norman will not climb down until he sees him take a mouthful. He looks away and Gonzales tries to slide the bread through the bars. Norman stops him.

NORMAN: Don't try me, old man.

Gonzales eats another morsel. Norman climbs down, shaking his head.

NORMAN: Look at this place. No windows since God was a boy, when the rain falls, it blows in. Rusty old beds. If I didn't take the sheets home, they would never get washed. What you say, Gonzales: wouldn't you like to go where you can eat proper food? Little boil yam and green banana, dumplings that sit heavy in your belly, stew chicken so tender it dropping off the bone? And talk to some new people? See a woman's soft face, Shakespeare, or walk through the hills without a soul to bother you, Dappo? When it comes right down to it, why would anyone want to stay in a place like this?

The patients have never heard him talk like this before. They begin to get agitated. Shakespeare buries his nose in his book, but keeps having to break off the make sure his slippers are in the right place. Dappo lies curled around his bread, eating it and watching the others, especially Norman, very intently. Gonzales begins rocking and singing.

GONZALES: (*Sings*) I going away on a sailing ship
                     And if I don't come back…
                     And if I don't come back…

NORMAN: Right. Key game time. You ready?

None of them are taking him on.

NORMAN: You know the rules. If you get the key, you can go out. I won't ask you where you going, or where you was when you come back.

Still they just look at him. Norman walks around the ward, dangling the key near to them. No takers.

Then each patient tries a strategy to get the key. Dappo decides that it is a like a game of stuckie (catch) and darts around Norman but goes back to a safe place on the wall when he fails to get the key. Gonzales fishes for the key, trying to get unobtrusively close enough to pinch it. Shakespeare tries to get Norman to join in a recitation of a poem as a way of distracting him so he can take it.

SHAKESPEARE: Here's one that a man like you ought to appreciate. (*Quoting*) Let me not to the marriage of true minds/ Admit impediments. Love is not love /which alters when it alteration finds,/or bends with the remover…

Shakespeare edges closer to the key, grabbing at it.

SHAKESPEARE: …to remove!

Norman easily eludes him. Shakespeare sees it is futile and retires.

SHAKESPEARE: O, no. It is an ever-fixed mark.

None of these strategies work and when Norman sees that they are all less stressed, he ends the game.

NORMAN: Nice try, gentlemen. Almost got me, but not quite. Never mind. Next time.

He puts the key back on his belt and goes to sit at his desk while the patients return to their beds, Dappo to mutter to himself, Shakespeare to read his book, Gonzales to polish the pebbles.

SCENE TWO

2 a.m. The ward is in darkness. The door is unlocked and Norman enters. He is tipsy and holds a tiny torch with which he lights his way to his desk. He trips and stumbles a few times, shushing himself when he does so. He seats himself at the desk and, after a while, begins looking in the drawers.

Like the eye adjusting to the shadows, the lights creep up so we eventually see that Gonzales is in his usual place in the window. He watches Norman from his perch with great stillness, then climbs down and goes over to him.

GONZALES: You find it?

NORMAN: What the fuck is wrong with you? Creeping up on people like a duppy.

Gonzales makes to turn away.

NORMAN: G, come back here. Come on, old man. Don't hold a grudge. I thought I left my wallet here, that's all.

GONZALES: Liquor.

NORMAN: So what? A man can't take a drink now and then? Nothing wrong with that.

GONZALES: You bought liquor.

NORMAN: Yes, I bought liquor. So what if... oh. You caught me, G. I had money on me. I didn't need my wallet. Don't know why I came back here.

Gonzales goes to return to his perch.

NORMAN: When you going to get too old to look out of that window, Gonzales?

Movement from Shakespeare's bed.

NORMAN: You awake there, poet?

No reply. Norman goes to turn on the light.

GONZALES: No.

NORMAN: Just checking. Old habits die hard.

Norman turns on the light. Shakespeare is humping the mattress and silently crying as if his heart is breaking.

NORMAN: Jesus.

Norman goes to wake Shakespeare. Gonzales stops him.

GONZALES: Leave him.

Norman turns the light back off.

GONZALES: He never wakes. Always cries. When he sleeps, he can't control himself.

NORMAN: Nothing much passes you, does it, old man. You see it all.

GONZALES: I see you.

NORMAN: Nothing to see, G. A foolish man wasting his time doing a job that no one appreciates for little and no money. Nothing to see.

GONZALES: I see you.

NORMAN: I used to be a shining example. "Bright boy, Norman. He going to go far", the men would sit in the rum shop of a Friday night and agree. A Q of white rum, and young Norman got a scholarship to high school in town: these were their two certainties in life. Yes, sir, that boy going to go far.

GONZALES: And this madhouse is where you reach?

Gonzales curls up and sits watching and listening to Norman intently.

NORMAN: Now you understanding things, Gonzales. O levels? Not a problem. Passed seven. A levels? Couldn't concentrate. The words slid off the page. Barely passed one. So no university. But I wanted to help, to be of service. That was the romance of the seventies, G. A man could make a difference. A good man could change the world. So I decided to become a psychiatric nurse, do my bit for the betterment of humanity.

GONZALES: Sometimes is hard to be a good man.

NORMAN: You right, G. Liquor can make a man chat fart sometimes.

Gonzales gets up to leave.

NORMAN: What about you, Gonzales? What do you think about up there on your perch?

GONZALES: The sea.

NORMAN: You don't fool me with that one.

GONZALES: I talk with an old friend of mine. He wants me to come and visit him.

NORMAN: And leave us? You can't do that.

GONZALES: He offers peace.

NORMAN: Doesn't the medication help?

GONZALES: Like grease on a glass window: it just makes him harder to see. He never goes away.

NORMAN: That's the difference between you and me, Gonzales. My back is broad. I can take a beating. If anything happened to this job, I would just make a new life for myself, find something else to do. I don't see death as a friend. As far as I am concerned, wanting death is accepting defeat.

GONZALES: Yes.

NORMAN: Wrong answer. You can't give up, G. You have to fight. That's what my wife used to say. If we wanted the good life, we had to fight for it. How could we go back to the district with our heads held high when, between the two of us, we didn't earn enough to keep the bailiff from our door? Fight for the good life. She gave up teaching. Three years of training. Gave it up. Sold insurance. And she made good money. Wanted me to do the same. To take the shame out of her eye.

GONZALES: That sounds like a life.

NORMAN: It does, doesn't it. I should go home.

GONZALES: Yes.

Norman gets up to go then turns back to Gonzales.

NORMAN: Do you remember Jimmy? Thin fellow, manic depressive, one crooked eye? Ward 13, the one they closed last year. I saw him tonight. They stoned him for stealing in the market. Two mangoes, they said. One wasn't even ripe. A stone struck him near the temple. Gone.

GONZALES: I don't remember him.

NORMAN: He wasn't anybody.

GONZALES: You should go home.

NORMAN: You're right. And you should get some rest.

Norman picks up the torch. As he leaves the ward, he shines it briefly at Dappo and the now still Shakespeare, checking they are all right. Gonzales goes to his bed.

ACT TWO

SCENE ONE

A few days later.

It is immediately obvious that the patients are less medicated and the nurse is more stressed. Norman, sweating and puffing, is pursuing Dappo around the ward. Dappo is shouting aggressively. Shakespeare is repeatedly placing and replacing his slippers by the side of his bed, then rocking and rubbing his hands. He looks thinner, tired. Gonzales alone looks the same, sitting on his bed, looking at the stones.

NORMAN: Enough! I can't keep this up, Dappo.

DAPPO: (*Standing on his bed*) The time for the mission is drawing nearer, fool. You can't stop me. If you stand in my way the wrath of God will come down on you, you get me?

NORMAN: Anything you say, Dappo. Just done the shouting.

SHAKESPEARE: How can I get anything done like this? Peasant.

DAPPO: What you have to do, bwoy?

NORMAN: I said enough, Dappo.

DAPPO: They told me I don't have to put up with him calling me names. They told me.

NORMAN: You hearing the voices again?

SHAKESPEARE: They are so loud, *I* can hear them. Even his delusions are coarse.

NORMAN: And you, stop provoking him.

SHAKESPEARE: I want to go. I want to leave this place. I missed my wedding because of this place. She might still be out there. Waiting.

DAPPO: Who, Mistress Mattress?

SHAKESPEARE: (*Shouting at Dappo*) She loved me. You don't know her. She loved me. I got sick, I am sick, it's the sickness that drove her away.

DAPPO: Fucking idiot.

Gonzales lies down and curls himself into a ball on his bed. Norman goes over to him.

NORMAN: You all right, G?

Gonzales turns away from him.

NORMAN: These madmen upsetting you?

GONZALES: The sea. Please.

NORMAN: You could fall and hurt yourself.

Gonzales turns away again. Norman is uncertain what to do.

GONZALES: Please.

NORMAN: What the hell. When they close this ward, I'm not going to have a job anyway, am I? Come on, old man.

Norman helps Gonzales up to his perch at the window. Gonzales pressed his face to the bars.

SHAKESPEARE: Close the ward?

NORMAN: What?

SHAKESPEARE: You said they going to close the ward.

NORMAN: Did I?

Shakespeare is very distressed. His rituals become faster, more intense. Dappo watches him in amusement.

DAPPO: (*To the voices*) Weak. Weak as water. No use on a mission, a man like that.

Dappo drops and immediately begins to do sit-ups, press-ups, staring aggressively at Shakespeare who goes anxiously to his book for comfort.

SHAKESPEARE: Tomorrow and tomorrow and tomorrow creeps in its petty pace from day to day…

DAPPO: Shut up! Fucking idiot.

SHAKESPEARE: Tomorrow and tomorrow and tomorrow.

Norman realizes what is happening behind him and comes down, bringing Gonzales down with him. He puts Gonzales to sit on his bed then turns to Dappo and Shakespeare.

NORMAN: You too. Both of you, sit. Sit!

He forcibly brings Shakespeare and Dappo to sit at the ends of their beds.

NORMAN: Can't avoid it any longer, so I might as well tell you men the truth. They are going to close the ward. That's why they needed your details, to find somebody they can release you in care of.

I mean, this place was built when they thought you all were lunatics, howling at the moon. They wouldn't lock you up if you had cancer would they?

Nothing to worry about. This is a not a problem, it is a challenge. That is what the administrator told me. A challenge.

There is a long silence as each man takes in the news.

SHAKESPEARE: Quite. Well, I should never have stayed here in the first place. I don't really belong. Not like them.

DAPPO: Them who? Who you fucking calling them? When they was building this place, you was standing around waiting to get in, 'bout you don't belong.

Gonzales has gone back to his perch and watches all their reactions. He seems almost content.

NORMAN: Look, times are hard all round. They are going to get harder. We have to face it. You understand what I am saying to you?

DAPPO: Name, rank and serial number.

NORMAN: No, no, this is not a plot. This is reality. You are going to have to go back to the hills.

DAPPO: (*To the voices*) Stop telling me that! I know, I know. Stop!

SHAKESPEARE: He can't go anywhere. He's mad. You must see that.

NORMAN: What about you, Shakespeare?

SHAKESPEARE: Whenever you say the world. In fact, I wondered if I might prevail upon you to lend me the money to purchase a small holdall for my possessions? I have things to do, people to see, you see. I'm ready.

He gets up to begin his ritual with his slippers and book again, but Norman stops him.

NORMAN: Who? Who do you have to see?

SHAKESPEARE: I'm an educated man. I can still find a wife.

NORMAN: Not a job, or a place to live? A wife, Shakespeare?

SHAKESPEARE: What is finer than love? When two hearts intertwine, when love makes your decisions…

Dappo gestures graphically to suggest fucking.

SHAKESPEARE: Baboon.

NORMAN: Gonzales, come down and join us.

Gonzales does not move.

NORMAN: Please. The sea not going anywhere. Come down.

Gonzales comes down and sits on his bed.

NORMAN: When last did any of you go to therapy?

DAPPO: Therapy?

SHAKESPEARE: That went with the cutbacks before last. May, 1989. Some years before you even got here, Dappo.

NORMAN: Right. Well, we are going to start our own group here.

SHAKESPEARE: You might have to explain the concept to him.

DAPPO: Don't do me any fucking favours.

The patients all walk away. Norman rounds them up and reseats them.

NORMAN: What else have you got to do? Come on.

DAPPO: We can talk about anything, right?

NORMAN: Why not.

DAPPO: You hear that, Mister Mattress?

SHAKESPEARE: This is not a good idea.

NORMAN: We are going to have to leave this place. This hospital has been occupying prime real estate and the ministry is going to tear it down to build harbourside town houses. All the other wards have been demolished. It'll soon be our turn. So you men need to be as strong as possible before we go out into the world.

SHAKESPEARE: I told you. I'm ready to go. I know my way around.

NORMAN: How much is bus fare?

SHAKESPEARE: Thruppence.

NORMAN: Dollars and cents now, my friend.

SHAKESPEARE: I knew that. Of course I did.

Shakespeare begins to rub his hands though the smile stays on his face.

SHAKESPEARE: I'm ready to go.

NORMAN: We need some ground rules.

Gonzales gets up to go to the window again, but Norman restrains him gently.

NORMAN: Everyone has to tell the truth. Everyone can ask whatever they want to ask. Everyone has to participate.

DAPPO: Any question?

NORMAN: Any.

SHAKESPEARE: Even you?

NORMAN: (*Amused*) Even me.

SHAKESPEARE: What does it feel like to have a wife? Is her skin soft in the morning?

NORMAN: It used to be, I think.

SHAKESPEARE: Used to?

NORMAN: She doesn't let me touch her any more. Said I wasn't ambitious enough, working at a mental hospital. Couldn't buy a house. She used to ask what is a man and wife without house and land.

DAPPO: Bitch.

GONZALES: She loved you?

NORMAN: Once, so she said. Then she got her visa to go to the US. To clean rich people's houses and make that good money she always talking about. So she can buy her own house.

DAPPO: I want to know about Shakespeare's wedding.

NORMAN: Maybe we should start with something less significant.

DAPPO: Then I am not playing.

SHAKESPEARE: This is not a game.

DAPPO: (*To voices*) Secrets. Dangerous things, secrets. Hiding.

NORMAN: Right, gentlemen. Shakespeare, why don't you tell us about your wedding.

SHAKESPEARE: Start with him (*pointing to Gonzales*). He never says anything. He has the most to hide.

NORMAN: He may not be ready yet.

SHAKESPEARE: Then I am not ready either.

DAPPO: I knew it. There never was a wedding. Nothing. No woman.

SHAKESPEARE: She was there. Waiting on me. Rice, bouquet, flowers, girl, everything. She was there.

NORMAN: So why didn't you get married?

SHAKESPEARE: I tried. I did everything. I tried everything I could think of.

DAPPO: Lie. She left you at the altar. Dumped your English-literature-quoting backside all over the chapel floor. Yes!

NORMAN: We are here to listen. Not pass judgement.

SHAKESPEARE: Every time I tried…

Shakespeare cannot bear sitting still anymore. He begins smoothing the corners of his bed, reaching for his slippers. Dappo grabs them away.

SHAKESPEARE: They brought me to the hospital. Admitted me to the acute ward. She wouldn't even talk to me for two weeks. Then she came to say she had sold the wedding dress and given the money to charity. Threw the bouquet at me. It was all dried up. Then I came here to Ward 11.

NORMAN: She wasn't the one for you.

SHAKESPEARE: What about him? What about David?

NORMAN: We were talking about you.

SHAKESPEARE: I want to know about him.

DAPPO: Not married.

SHAKESPEARE: When did you get sick?

DAPPO: People don't understand me. A prophet without honour.

SHAKESPEARE: He's mad.

NORMAN: Ill.

SHAKESPEARE: I'm ill. He's sad. And that lout is mad.

DAPPO: If you hold a man by his neck tight enough for long enough, he dies.

NORMAN: Enough, Dappo.

GONZALES: And you don't even need to touch him. You can do it with this. The mind. I've seen it.

NORMAN: What have you seen, Dappo?

DAPPO: How they break people. How they suck the life out of people. I've seen it.

NORMAN: When did you see it?

DAPPO: Herne Hill. (*To voices*) I have to tell the truth. That's the rules.

NORMAN: Dappo? Listen to me, Dappo. Can you hear me? What did you see?

DAPPO: Kneeling.

NORMAN: Who was kneeling, Dappo?

DAPPO: Name, rank and serial number.

SHAKESPEARE: He's just making things up. He's not playing fair. He just wants you to pay attention to him.

NORMAN: And you don't?

SHAKESPEARE: I'm ready to leave. At a moment's notice. Out of here, into the wide world.

GONZALES: Tired.

Gonzales curls up on his bunk in the foetal position.

NORMAN: All right. I think we've all had enough. We'll try this again tomorrow.

SHAKESPEARE: Tomorrow and tomorrow and tomorrow…

NORMAN: I don't think we have all that many tomorrows left, teacher. Can I trust all of you to behave yourselves for half an hour? There is something I need to do.

DAPPO: What?

SHAKESPEARE: The concept of privacy means nothing to you, does it, Dappo. If he doesn't want to tell us what he is doing, he doesn't have to. Do you?

NORMAN: A letter. I need to write a letter to the Minister of Health.

SHAKESPEARE: Ah.

DAPPO: Write to the Prime Minister. He is a friend of mine.

NORMAN: I'm going to invite him to come and visit us, let him meet you fellows. Maybe then he won't be so quick to close this ward down.

SHAKESPEARE: I'll be happy to draft it for you. Or proofread your effort, perhaps? Any assistance I can offer, of course.

NORMAN: Thanks, Shakespeare, but I think I can manage this one.

SCENE TWO

The ward has been tidied, somewhat. A rather sad banner with the words WARD 11 WELCOMES THE MINISTER hangs over the doorway. All three patients are dressed after a fashion and sitting on their beds, staring at Norman who is pacing, agitatedly.

NORMAN: So we all understand what is going to happen here today? Dappo?

DAPPO: Minister of Health is coming to visit.

NORMAN: And we need to impress him, don't we. What are we going to tell him about our life on this ward? Shakespeare?

SHAKESPEARE: May I say that perhaps we should take this opportunity to explain the dire social consequences of the breakdown of traditional family structures...

NORMAN: No! No, Shakespeare. Not this time. Remember what we talked about?

SHAKESPEARE: We are not ready to go back into the community. There are a few lifeskills we still need to learn.

NORMAN: Good, good.

SHAKESPEARE: But isn't that a little dishonest? I mean, I could walk through that door and survive out there tomorrow.

NORMAN: Say it for Gonzales, Shakespeare. Okay?

SHAKESPEARE: And Dappo.

DAPPO: Don't do one fucking thing for me, teacher.

NORMAN: Sit. I said, sit! Right. He is going to be here any moment now. You all right there old man?

Gonzales is lost, staring at his pebbles.

NORMAN: Stay with us just for a few minutes, G.

No response from Gonzales

NORMAN: You smell the sea breeze starting to blow? That little cool breeze? You feel it?

Gonzales looks up and smiles.

NORMAN: That's right. That smile is worth gold.

SHAKESPEARE: Silver and gold have I none...

DAPPO: No fucking sense, either.

SHAKESPEARE: Intelligence! I have intelligence.

DAPPO: CIA. They have a file on me, did you know that? You didn't know that. Follow everything I do. Spy on me even when I am sleeping.

SHAKESPEARE: Are you going to tell the Minister that?

There is a loud knock on the ward door. Norman straightens his uniform nervously.

NORMAN: Right, gentlemen. On your best behaviour. Remember we are fighting for our lives here.

Norman opens the ward door, unlocking it and then flinging it open with a flourish. There is a large envelope with an elaborate gold seal on the steps. Not a soul in sight. Norman looks around. Nothing. He takes up the envelope and brings it back into the ward. Gonzales, seeing the ward door open, tries to ease towards it. Norman relocks the door before he can get there. He carries the envelope over to his desk, puts it down, and then stands looking at it.

The others come to join him, staring at the letter.

SHAKESPEARE: I always said politicians were paper tigers.

DAPPO: You not going to open it?

NORMAN: Of course I am.

They still stand and stare. Gonzales eventually opens it, holds it at arms' length, and reads it. Folds it and puts it back in the envelope.

NORMAN: So?

GONZALES: The minister has been called away on urgent cabinet business and regrets he is unable to visit your establishment as organized. He wishes you all the very best for the future.

Norman grabs the letter and reads it himself.

Shakespeare looks at it over his shoulder.

SHAKESPEARE: They spelt organized wrong. It is z not s.

NORMAN: I need to think.

DAPPO: Write him again. (*To voices*) I'm not ready yet. I still have to train some more. Not yet!

SHAKESPEARE: It seems we are in a bit of a pickle. Up the proverbial creek.

NORMAN: Gentlemen, please. I need to decide what my next move is going to be.

GONZALES: Hector's River. On the north coast.

They ignore him.

GONZALES: I lived there. Fished off the beach. Hector's River.

Norman realizes what the old man is doing and quickly gets his files out of his desk.

NORMAN: So now you decide to tell me where you come from. Hector's River. Any family there?

GONZALES: I had a wife; she is dead now.

SHAKESPEARE: You? You had a wife?

NORMAN: No time for that now, Shakespeare. No one else, Gonzales?

GONZALES: No. I had a boat. Probably stolen by now.

NORMAN: Any property?

GONZALES: The house burnt down.

DAPPO: It talks!

SHAKESPEARE: What was she like, your wife?

GONZALES: She is dead.

SHAKESPEARE: I know, but what was she like before she died?

GONZALES: She is dead.

Gonzales goes back to his bed. Shakespeare goes after him but Norman restrains him.

DAPPO: You see? He is not playing by the rules. He was supposed to tell the truth, answer any questions we asked. Nobody tells you the truth.

NORMAN: Leave him alone, Dappo.

SHAKESPEARE: Where is Herne Hill, Dappo?

DAPPO: London, ignoramus. London. (*To voices*) How could he know? He doesn't know.

SHAKESPEARE: When were you there, David?

DAPPO: Dappo. My name is Dappo.

Dappo is getting very angry.

SHAKESPEARE: He has to tell the truth. Doesn't he have to tell the truth?

NORMAN: When we agree, yes.

SHAKESPEARE: I agree now. Gonzales?

GONZALES: Yes.

NORMAN: Come, Dappo. Fair's fair. You asked the questions last time.

Dappo reluctantly comes to take his seat with the others.

NORMAN: Who gave you that name?

DAPPO : I took it.

NORMAN: Who from?

DAPPO: Dappo.

SHAKESPEARE: It can't be from the word dapper because you are anything but. It can't be from the word a*dap*table, because you have been the same ignoramus ever since you came on this ward...

NORMAN: Let Dappo tell us, please.

DAPPO: Dappo. He was the hardest man I ever saw. Telephone cut from ear to mouth corner. Kill a man and don't blink. Hard like rockstone.

NORMAN: And where did you meet him?

DAPPO: When I lived in Herne Hill, innit.

SHAKESPEARE: He hears voices. Why would you believe anything he says?

GONZALES: Who did he kill?

DAPPO: People. People cast their eyes down when he stepped onto the train. Fraid to catch his eye. No one sat beside him. He cleaned his nails with a hunting knife. Three gold teeth.

SHAKESPEARE: And you encountered this vision of loveliness in London?

NORMAN: Let him talk, Shakespeare.

DAPPO: I lived there. Eight years, I lived there. My mother sent for me when I was nine. Sent a suit for me to travel in, everything. Flew in to Heathrow, a name tag pinned on my suit. Didn't recognize her at first, my mum. And the man. He was there too.

NORMAN: Your father?

DAPPO: Him? Never. (*To voices*) So what if they know? Why shouldn't I tell them?

NORMAN: Who was he, the man that met you at the airport? Was he Dappo?

DAPPO: (*Laughs*) Dappo? Dappo would kill him and leave his body in the street with one eye open.

NORMAN: Is that what you wanted to do to him?

DAPPO: (*Becoming his stepfather*) I told your mother not to send for you. You have no bleeding use, brought up running wild in the bush.

NORMAN: Dappo?

DAPPO: Three schools and you've been expelled from all three.

Can't read, can't write, can't conduct yourself like a civilised human being...

NORMAN: (*Playing Dappo*) I'm sorry.

DAPPO: Sorry isn't good enough!

NORMAN: I'll do better next time.

DAPPO: What next time? We leave you to babysit your brother and sister and you leave the window open so they nearly freeze to death… Shut up when I am talking to you! You go to school and get into fights. You stay home from school and play nintendo instead of doing your chores? What use are you?

NORMAN: I am my mother's son.

DAPPO: Kneel down. I said kneel down in front of me. That's right. Now beg for my forgiveness. Beg! You call that begging? You call that begging?

Dappo starts to strike Norman with an imaginary stick.

DAPPO: Now look what you have made me do. Break your mother's broom. You're going to have to buy it back. School? You don't deserve to go to school. You better find yourself a job because you aren't eating in this house for free any more…

NORMAN: What does my mother have to say about this?

DAPPO: Your mother? She says what I tell her to say.

NORMAN: Doesn't she love me anymore?

DAPPO: The only reason she sent for you is because your grand-mother threatened to turn you out. And now I see why! Fucking waste of space.

SHAKESPEARE: Jesus.

NORMAN: Dappo. Time to stop now, Dappo.

DAPPO: You can take the boy out of the country, but you can't take the country out of the boy.

Gonzales goes over the Dappo and touches his shoulder. Dappo looks at him, then seems to come to his senses.

DAPPO: What? What the fuck you staring at?

SHAKESPEARE: Nothing. Nothing.

Dappo goes over and moves Shakespeare's slippers to provoke him. Shakespeare rushes over to put them back.

DAPPO: Who you feeling sorry for now? Bitch.

NORMAN: No need for that, Dappo.

DAPPO: Well, look at her. Fussing and fluttering and carrying on. (*He imitates Shakespeare's rituals*)

SHAKESPEARE: I could get married. Any time I wanted to. Leave this place and get married just like that.

DAPPO: Who would fucking have you?

SHAKESPEARE: I could get married if I wanted!

DAPPO: So why don't you *want* to then?

Shakespeare begins smoothing and folding and placing and replacing his slippers. The atmosphere is very tense. Dappo is delighted.

NORMAN: Enough.

DAPPO: I didn't start it.

Dappo whistles "Here Comes The Bride"

NORMAN: I said, enough! Session over for today.

Norman takes off the ward door key and puts it on his desk. He pretends to get out some files and work on them. The patients gradually creep towards the key, freezing every time he looks up, feigning disinterest. It is like a game of red light. Just as Shakespeare is about to grab the key, Norman casually takes it up and puts it back on his belt.

SCENE THREE

Evening. Norman enters the ward. He is not wearing his uniform and is carrying a large bag. He is in a good mood, almost too good. None of the patients pay him much mind.

NORMAN: Well, don't just sit there. Come and help me with all this.

SHAKESPEARE: You're not supposed to be here now. Your shift is over.

NORMAN: These are changing times. Rules can be broken. Don't just sit around.

SHAKESPEARE: But…

DAPPO: What's in the bag?

NORMAN: Come and see.

Norman sets down the bag and they gradually come round to take a look at what is in it. He produces a set of drums, party hats, noisemakers. The patients look dubious.

NORMAN: Come on, gentlemen. Get into the spirit of things.

SHAKESPEARE: What things exactly?

NORMAN: You've been here too long. Perhaps you think life outside this ward is frightening, that it is better to be in here. I wanted you to know there are good times to be had in the world.

Norman pulls the patients into a circle and puts their party hats on them. They sit with the hats on, looking at each other. After consideration, Dappo takes Gonzales's hat and put it on. He puts his hat on Gonzales. Shakespeare takes his hat off and takes a long look at it, smoothing where the paper is folded. Then he reluctantly puts it back on. Gonzales finds a noisemaker and plays with it.

NORMAN: Right. How about a game? A song? Come on, fellows. We looking to have a good time.

He dances a few steps, smiling broadly. The patients look at one another growing more and more uncomfortable with Norman's behaviour. Shakespeare takes off his hat.

NORMAN: Put the fucking hat on, all right?

Shakespeare puts it back on, but begins one of his rituals, going at speed and flustering himself and having to start all over.

NORMAN: Come on, Dappo. You must have been to a party when you were a little boy.

DAPPO: *(To voices)* I don't know why. I don't know why!

NORMAN: Come on. Somebody. This is a celebration, for God's sake. Tell you what. A song will break the ice. A nice lively one, one we all know.

Norman begins to sing "Three Little Birds". Gonzales claps along, Dappo joins in, and Shakespeare bobs a little to the beat. Norman looks pleased and repeats the song, teaching them the words, then leads them in a final lively chorus which they seem to enjoy.

NORMAN: That's more like it. Now we getting somewhere. Okay, who next? Who has a song we can sing?

Gonzales goes over to the drum and strokes the skin. It makes a soft sound, like a moan. He pulls back.

NORMAN: That's right, G. Make some noise. Let them know that we are still here. Go on.

Dappo grabs the drum and begins banging on it wildly. Shakespeare cringes.

NORMAN: Give it to me, Dappo. It is not a toy.

Dappo dances out of reach, banging on the drum.

DAPPO: 'Cause every little thing is gonna be all right...

NORMAN: Now, Dappo.

DAPPO: This is my message to you... oo... oo

Dappo hops around the ward, tormenting the others. Norman realizes he is ruining any progress he has made and gets angry.

NORMAN: Give me the drum.

DAPPO: Don't worry about a thing!

Norman grabs Dappo by the waist of his trousers, takes the drum from him and lets him go with a shove.

NORMAN: Don't try me tonight, boy. You can push a man too far.

Dappo stands defiant as Norman fights to control his temper. Shakespeare watches fearfully. There is a major, physical confrontation brewing until Dappo drops and starts to do push ups, staring aggressively at Norman. Norman's aggression drains away at so absurd a sight.

NORMAN: When God made your three, he threw away the moulds. Is it too much to ask that you all at least try to behave normally?

Gonzales walks over and takes up the drums and begins to play. He is a little rusty but soon gets into his stride. The sound is strong without being loud. Norman recognizes the rhythm he is playing and begins to move to it.

NORMAN: That's right, old man. That's right. You sound like one of those men who used to come to play at every nine night celebration in our district. Play and sing for the dead from sunset to sunrise. Keep a little salt in the bottom of their pockets, so that they could drink plenty white rum.

Dappo watches Norman. Norman seeing this, pulls him into the dance.

NORMAN: Your grandmother never took you to a nine night, Dappo? You never hear the drum play so long that you think is your own heartbeat?

Dappo begins to move. Gonzales closes his eyes and begins to hum and then to sing.

GONZALES: If I had the wings of a dove,
If I had the wings of a dove,
I would fly
Fly away.

NORMAN: Fly away
And be at rest.

GONZALES: Since I have no wings
Since I have no wings
Since I have no wings
I cannot fly, fly, fly, fly

NORMAN: Since I have no wings
Since I have no wings
Since I have no wings
I'm gonna sing, sing, sing, sing.

Norman and Gonzales repeat the song and this time Dappo joins in with growing confidence. Norman begins to dance, showing Dappo the moves. Dappo does his own version.

NORMAN: What happen, Shakespeare? Come, man.

SHAKESPEARE: I don't know the lyrics, I'm afraid.

NORMAN: This isn't literature, Shakespeare. This is life. Everybody knows the words.

Shakespeare allows himself to be drawn into the song and dance, awkward and self-aware. Dappo is lost in the music. Gonzales's drumming becomes more and more confident and intricate. They stop and listen when, eyes closed, he begins to play a solo. When he finishes, they applaud. He smiles, but it fades as soon as he opens his eyes. He puts down the drums.

NORMAN: Come on, old man. Stay with us for a while. You have magic in those hands. Where did you learn?

GONZALES: I played for my own mother's nine night. She died when I was eleven years old.

NORMAN: I'm sorry. Life is a cruel thing sometimes.

DAPPO: (*Loudly*) If I had the wings of a dove…

SHAKESPEARE: Inappropriate, Dappo.

DAPPO: Fuck you.

NORMAN: All right, gentlemen. Simmer down. Smile, remember? Happy times. What about another song?

Gonzales takes up the drum again and starts to play again. This time he sings, a traditional nine-night song.

GONZALES: A pair of every animal was saved in the ark
Saved in the ark
Saved in the ark
A pair of every animal was saved in the ark
Keyman lock the door and gone.

Keyman, Keyman,
Fi mi bredda Keyman,
Keyman lock the door and gone.

Keyman, Keyman
Fi mi bredda, Keyman
Keyman lock di door and gone.

Gonzales puts down the drum

GONZALES: Keyman lock the door and gone.

NORMAN: You think I am the keyman? I not going anywhere. See? I am here with you.

DAPPO: Keyman, Keyman, Keyman lock the door and gone.

NORMAN: Stop that, Dappo.

GONZALES: So open the door then nuh, Keyman?

NORMAN: You would go.

GONZALES: Isn't that what you want?

NORMAN: Not just like that. With nowhere to go, no one to see to you.

Gonzales turns away and goes back to his bed.

DAPPO: Keyman lock the door and gone.

NORMAN: Not now, Dappo!

Dappo too turns away.

DAPPO: (*To voices*) Trying to soften me up, trying to get under my guard. Not fooling me. Never.

SHAKESPEARE: Is it over? May I take this hat off now?

NORMAN: You know what, Shakespeare? Do whatever the fuck you please. All of you. Do whatever the fuck you please.

Gonzales returns to his perch. The others take off their hats and go back to their beds, Shakespeare to his rituals. Norman is left standing alone in the middle of the ward. None of them will meet his eye. He kisses his teeth, repacks the bag, and leaves the ward.

ACT THREE

SCENE ONE

Early Evening

Things have truly fallen apart on Ward 11. There is no medication, so all the patients are acting up. Norman, looking more than a little desperate, tries to keep order.

DAPPO: How am I to train on a hungry belly? Empty bag can't stand up, man.

NORMAN: I talked to the guys in the kitchen. They said they would send food today. Promised faithfully. That's the best I can do.

SHAKESPEARE: Why didn't you bring us some? You did yesterday. Why not today?

NORMAN: A slight disagreement with my bank. They didn't want to give me any money to buy it with.

DAPPO: They are always fighting against black people.

NORMAN: I think they noticed I haven't been paid for the last month.

SHAKESPEARE: How do they expect us to maintain any semblance of a decent life under these conditions? Incomprehensible.

NORMAN: Short answer is they don't. They don't expect anything from us. You all right there, old man?

Gonzales does not look up from his stones.

SHAKESPEARE: He has not spoken for three days.

DAPPO: Fucking idiot.

SHAKESPEARE: Be silent!

DAPPO: Two fucking idiots.

NORMAN: Gentlemen, please. I don't have the strength for this today.

A loud knock on the ward door.

NORMAN: At last. Stomach at the ready, boys. It's chow time. You too, Gonzales.

Norman opens the ward doors, the others peering over his shoulder eagerly. There is nothing but another large envelope on the steps.

NORMAN: (*Shouts*) Very funny. Ha, ha, ha. Now bring on the food.

Nothing happens.

NORMAN: Hungry patients here, man. Stop the foolishness.

Still nothing. Norman takes up the envelope, turns it over. Gonzales, seeing that the door is open, makes for it. He nearly makes it but Norman stops him. Gonzales goes immediately back to his bed. Norman locks the door and carries the letter back to his desk where he reads it, folds it, then unfolds it and reads it again.

Shakespeare goes into his compulsive behaviour in overdrive. Dappo watches him for a while then stops him by holding his hands still. Shakespeare struggles against him for a while then quiets and goes limp. He is about to lean on Dappo when the younger man throws him off.

DAPPO: (*To voices*) Shut up! Shut up. I couldn't stand the fidgeting, okay. That's the only reason I touched him. Look at him. What could he do to me?

Shakespeare goes back to smoothing, sitting, standing with a vengeance.

Norman becomes so still that the patients notice: first Gonzales, then Dappo then Shakespeare.

GONZALES: Is it time?

Norman doesn't answer. Instead he stands and faces them. He takes off the ward key, shows it to them all and then hangs it on his waist. The challenge is clear. The patients realize the Key Game is on and begin to play it, but halfheartedly.

NORMAN: All these years, you've been in this ward and you've never figured out how to get this key from me? What are you? Lunatics? Madmen? Retards?

The patients begin to get annoyed.

NORMAN: Not on brain cell between the three of you. All of us locked in this place: one of me and three of you and you still can't figure out how to get this key from me.

In the distance, the sound of bulldozers starting up.

NORMAN: Poor little Gilbert, got left by a woman at the altar, hiding away in this place. Hell hath no fury, Gilbert. You're better off alone, boyee. You and the mattress.

Shakespeare really goes for the key.

NORMAN: What are the voices saying to you today, refugee? Cold weather mad you in England and you run come home to the sun? Stinking little schizo.

DAPPO: Man on a mission now. On a mission.

Dappo too really goes for the key.

NORMAN: What about you, fisherman? No more fish to fry? You think you're the only man who has lost a wife? You think you're the only person whose house burned down? Get up and do something, damn you.

Gonzales looks up and focuses on Norman. They are all hurt and angry. They round on Norman, working together in the Key Game for the first time.

NORMAN: Finally figured it out, have you?

They all charge Norman together and take the key from him forcibly, hurting him in the process. They go in triumph to the door of ward and put the key in the door. The sound of the bulldozers grows louder. They realize that Norman is not trying to stop them and hesitate before opening the door.

GONZALES: Just easy so? We win so easy?

NORMAN: How could I win the key game against all three of you?

SHAKESPEARE: To the victor, the spoils.

Gonzales goes back and takes the envelope off Norman's desk. He reads it, then goes to Norman and helps him to his feet.

SHAKESPEARE: What? What does it say?

Dappo joins Shakespeare reading the letter.

SHAKESPEARE: Demolition day.

DAPPO: When?

SHAKESPEARE: Today.

DAPPO: He let us win, man!

They all go back to tend to Norman, putting him to sit on one of the beds. They all sit with him and give him back the key.

SHAKESPEARE: They can't turn us out. They can't demolish the ward if we are still in it. That would be murder.

DAPPO: I don't have anywhere to go.

NORMAN: Maybe. Maybe you are right. Gonzales, what are they doing now?

Gonzales climbs to his window perch and looks out. The faint flashing of an orange light can be seen.

GONZALES: Just parked. Talking.

NORMAN: They are going to have to negotiate with us some-time. We will just have to wait them out.

Norman is obviously in some pain from the game. Shakespeare and then Dappo stay close to him. Both are fighting desperately hard to control their behaviours: Shakespeare sitting on his hands in his effort, Dappo putting his hands over his ears. The engines of the bulldozers are cut. There is an odd silence.

GONZALES: It looks like they going away.

SHAKESPEARE: That's good. Isn't that good?

NORMAN: For now. Yes. It's good.

SHAKESPEARE: It's good.

NORMAN: Whatever happens we can't stay here. You under-stand what I am saying to you, Shakespeare? Dappo?

SHAKESPEARE: But you don't have anywhere to go, do you, Dappo. You said so.

DAPPO: Didn't.

SHAKESPEARE: I heard you. We all did.

DAPPO: What you talking to me for? Why you always talking to me?

NORMAN: Would it be so bad to go back and live with your grandmother, Dappo?

DAPPO: Not before I complete my mission. After that, maybe.

NORMAN: Sometimes a mission can take a whole lifetime, Dappo. You have to live somewhere until it's over.

SHAKESPEARE: She can't turn you away. She is family to you.

DAPPO: (*To voices*) Nearest and dearest. Nearest and dearest. They hurt you the most, man.

NORMAN: Your grandmother cared enough to bring you here, so you could get help, Dappo. She didn't turn you out into the street.

DAPPO: She grew me. When they sent me back from London, she took me back into her house. But I couldn't fit everything into that life anymore. You get me?

SHAKESPEARE: You had grown up?

NORMAN: You had changed, Dappo.

DAPPO: She didn't respect my mission.

NORMAN: And the voices told you about your mission.

DAPPO: I knew what to do. I just needed to prepare. She wouldn't leave me alone to do what I had to do. After me to bathe and talking to me, talking to me, talking to me.

NORMAN: She committed you.

DAPPO: First she prayed over me. Sometimes she prayed so loud and so long, I thought she was another voice in my head. Burned me with Holy Water, dragged me into the church...

NORMAN: She wanted you to get well.

DAPPO: But I told her God knows about my mission. I told him about it from I was in London and he said it was all right. She didn't listen.

NORMAN: Tell us about your mission, Dappo.

DAPPO: I can't. (To voices) I didn't. I didn't tell!

SHAKESPEARE: Ask the voices.

GONZALES: The bulldozers are going away!

Shakespeare and Dappo celebrate. Gonzales comes down to join them.

NORMAN: What are we going to do, gentlemen? Make a run for it? Or wait?

SHAKESPEARE: We have rights. We're human. They can't bull-doze us out. I'm not going anywhere.

DAPPO: That's right.

There is short silence.

DAPPO: I'm hungry.

NORMAN: We all are.

Another short silence.

NORMAN: I need to figure out our next move.

SHAKESPEARE: Why should I have to move? If I want to stay here, I should be allowed to stay here.

NORMAN: We need more time, that's all. Right. I am going to leave you three alone for a little while. Can I trust you?

SHAKESPEARE: I have always been a model of rectitude.

DAPPO: A fucking pain in the rectitude, you mean.

NORMAN: I am serious, gentlemen. I am going to appeal to the men who have come to demolish the ward. They probably don't even know we are here. I'm going to go and talk to them. Open lines of communication. Establish a dialogue.

SHAKESPEARE: Ah. Appeal to their humanity. Good strategy. (*Quotes*) But I, being poor, have only my dreams;/I have spread my dreams under your feet;/ Tread softly because you tread on my dreams.

NORMAN: I am leaving the key in your charge, Shakespeare. Lock the door after I go. Do not open it for anyone but me.

DAPPO: I should get the key, man.

Norman gives the key to Shakespeare who follows him to the door and locks it behind him when he goes.

DAPPO: Give it to me. I should have it.

SHAKESPEARE: A modicum of respect for the graveness of the situation we are in would be appropriate right now, David.

DAPPO: Dappo!

SHAKESPEARE: Gonzales? What do you think? He gave the key to me. Am I the keyman now?

Gonzales nods.

SHAKESPEARE: I told you.

DAPPO: What does he know? He don't know nothing, man.

GONZALES: If I go to sea, I'll be all right.

DAPPO: How you going to go to sea without a boat, fisherman?

GONZALES: I'll be all right.

SHAKESPEARE: You going away on a sailing ship?

DAPPO: (*Sings*) Brown skin gal, stay home and mind baby…

SHAKESPEARE: Must you do that?

DAPPO: You don't complain when he sings it.

SHAKESPEARE: Because he has a reason for singing. You have a
reason for singing, don't you, Gonzales?

GONZALES: I used to sing it for her.

SHAKESPEARE: To your wife. See, I told you he had a reason.

GONZALES: Before I left to go fishing. When I heard she was
pregnant, I sang it even louder. Even while I was at sea. The sea
was never so loving, giving me fish whenever I asked. My heart
was so big and full, I thought a sea gull would see it and come
down and try and steal a piece.

DAPPO: Old man like you had a child? You don't look like a
cocksman.

GONZALES: It died.

SHAKESPEARE: I'm so sorry.

GONZALES: Because I beat her. It wasn't my child. When I was
away, another man had crept into our home. Raped her. She
didn't tell me because she knew I wouldn't go back to sea if she
did. And then she found out she was pregnant.

SHAKESPEARE: What did the police have to say about all this?

197

GONZALES: When you're at sea and it is flat calm, the sun tries to shine through it. But the sea protects herself and bounces that light back so bright it blinds you. Quick as a flash. Look at the sea the wrong way and you go blind.

DAPPO: You burnt down the house!

GONZALES: I sailed before daylight and left the lamp burning. She would not talk to me, look at me. It was the first time I had raised my hand to her. So I left the lamp burning so she would think about me as she blew it out in the dawn.

SHAKESPEARE: And the lamp caused the fire.

GONZALES: She is dead now.

SHAKESPEARE: How were you to know, Gonzales? It is not your fault.

GONZALES: She was the first person that stayed with me. She loved me. She cared for me. She was my heart.

DAPPO: Your heart is still beating in your chest, old man. You should listen to it sometimes.

GONZALES: It tells me to go to the sea. I took her body and went out to beyond the breakers and gave her to the sea so she would be rocked forever. When I got back they stoned me. Chased me. Said I had lost my mind, disrespecting her body. But I hadn't. I had just lost my soul.

SHAKESPEARE: You will find it again.

GONZALES: I am too old to keep looking.

He gets up and goes over to stand by the ward door.

SHAKESPEARE: I can't do it, Gonzales. He gave me the key so I could keep you safe.

GONZALES: Nowhere is safe from memory. You of all people should know that. These last days is like I can hear her voice calling to me. Sometimes life is more pain than it is worth.

Shakespeare unlocks the door and opens it.

DAPPO: I told him he should have given me the key. Weak as water. Weak as water.

Gonzales is standing at the threshold, staring into the night.

SHAKESPEARE: Where you going to go?

GONZALES: Sometimes at night the sea lightning shows me where she's resting. I see the fishing boats coming from the west every morning. I'll go that way and find where the boats come ashore.

He turns and comes back into the ward. He takes up his pebbles and gives them to Dappo. Dappo throws them away but Gonzales picks them up and returns them to him.

DAPPO: Gonzales, this isn't right, man.

GONZALES: Give them to him for me, when he gets back. Tell him thank you.

SHAKESPEARE: Perhaps Dappo is right, Gonzales. If you told him about what happened, if we tried to think it through…

GONZALES: Time for thinking pass now.

He walks out of the ward into the night.

DAPPO: (*To the voices*) Of course he'll come back. Where else has he got to go?

The power to the ward is cut and the lights go off. Shakespeare slams the door shut and locks it. Dappo tries the switch, but no joy. Moonlight through a window is the only illumination now.

SHAKESPEARE: They're just trying to scare us. Nothing to worry about.

Dappo begins to exercise furiously.

DAPPO: The final assault. Every man for himself. (*To voices*) I could be fit enough. Why not? I've trained.

Both men cower, as there is a loud banging on the door. Pause. Then more banging.

NORMAN: What is going on in there? Open this blasted door this minute.

SHAKESPEARE: I told you it was nothing to worry about.

Shakespeare lets Norman in. He is puffing and panting and drags Gonzales along behind him.

NORMAN: Five minutes. I leave you lot alone for five minutes and this is what happens?

He shoves Gonzales onto his bed and rounds on the other two.

NORMAN: I trusted you. I left the key with you. And you let Gonzales creep out to his death?

DAPPO: Is his fault. He did it.

SHAKESPEARE: He wanted to go. I couldn't think of a good reason to stop him in the circumstances.

GONZALES: Sail on the land breeze. Sweet as sugar.

Gonzales takes back his pebbles and gives them to Norman.

GONZALES: Hard to be a good man sometimes.

NORMAN: You going leave us in our darkest hour, Gonzales?

GONZALES: But you doing better than most.

Gonzales closes Norman's fingers around his pebbles.

NORMAN: I could stop you. I should stop you.

GONZALES: For what? When you hear my friend whispering outside the window, you just keep your mind on these.

Gonzales leaves. Dappo and Shakespeare walk behind him to near the door and watch him go. Norman looks at the pebbles, struggling to control his emotions. Then puts them in his pocket. He becomes his old, brisk self, takes the key back from Shakespeare and locks the door.

NORMAN: The old man is right. You can't stay here forever, gentlemen. This is a battle we can't win. We have to find the best way out of it that we can.

DAPPO: Don't let the moon overlook you. It will draw your spirit out of your body.

SHAKESPEARE: Superstitious nonsense.

DAPPO: Always have something to say. Always have some comment to make. You going dead in this place and is your mouth going kill you.

SHAKESPEARE: I am an educated man. I am a trained educator. Words are my ammunition, my sustenance. You wouldn't understand.

DAPPO: You chat too fucking much. This is war. Actions speak louder than words, man. This is war.

NORMAN: Quiet down, both of you.

SHAKESPEARE: What are they going to do with us? Did they tell you?

NORMAN: Those men are just doing as they are told. Obeying orders.

DAPPO: Soldiers. I told you it was fucking war.

SHAKESPEARE: I knew this time would come, of course. I knew I would have to leave. It's been a while. I may have to make a few readjustments.

Dappo climbs up to Gonzales's perch and looks out.

NORMAN: Maybe you could train to work with other people like yourself, Shakespeare. Make literature their new compulsion.

SHAKESPEARE: Obsession, not compulsion. A compulsion is something you have to do, you see, and you can't *do* literature. It must be appreciated, enjoyed. It must be an obsession.

NORMAN: See, a born educator.

DAPPO: Couldn't teach me a damn thing.

SHAKESPEARE: Pearl before swine. You have to have a hungry for knowledge.

201

DAPPO: I'm hungry till my lips are white. What you going to teach me?

SHAKESPEARE: What do you want to know?

DAPPO: If I knew it already, what would I need you for?

NORMAN: Sounds to me like you have a plan there, Shakespeare. Something to look forward to.

SHAKESPEARE: I loved teaching. The hairs stood up on the back of my neck when my third formers recited Wordsworth's Daffodils.

DAPPO: You ever see a frigging daffodil, teacher? I have. Nothing to it.

SHAKESPEARE: And then there were those particular students that make it all worthwhile. They told me I got too close, but how can you get too close to someone you are teaching and who teaches you about yourself?

DAPPO: A student?

SHAKESPEARE: A bright spirit. A shining star. They didn't understand that kind of closeness.

DAPPO: You were feeling up the girls in your class!

SHAKESPEARE: Rubbish. It was purely platonic. They wouldn't listen.

DAPPO: Dirty old man.

SHAKESPEARE: I was engaged, you idiot. And it wasn't a she, it was a he.

DAPPO: Dirty old batty man, then.

SHAKESPEARE: It takes a filthy, perverted little mind to jump to that conclusion. Look at me, I am an educated man. I live a blameless life. I helped him. He wanted to learn and I taught him. He wanted to understand the finer things in life and I polished him. They all just jumped to conclusions. And they confused him and he said I had touched him.

NORMAN: Was this before or after the wedding?

SHAKESPEARE: She understood everything when I explained it to her. We agreed that after we were married I wouldn't teach him any more. That marital love was the most important thing.

DAPPO: And how old was your toy boy, teacher?

NORMAN: Be quiet, Dappo.

DAPPO: Why should I be? It's plain as day he's as bent as a nine pound note. Couldn't marry her? Couldn't fuck her more like.

SHAKESPEARE: I'm warning you.

DAPPO: Come on then. Anytime you're ready. You and me.

SHAKESPEARE: Right.

Shakespeare and Dappo square off.

NORMAN: Stop this, the pair of you. We have far more serious problems to worry about.

Dappo ignores Norman and advances on Shakespeare.

DAPPO: About time we settled this, man. Where you going?

SHAKESPEARE: Do that again.

Shakespeare backs away and Dappo comes forward again.

DAPPO: You can run but you can't hide, fool.

SHAKESPEARE: You are walking forwards.

Dappo looks down at his own feet.

SHAKESPEARE: You got so angry at me that you walked forward.

Dappo looks to Norman who nods confirmation. Dappo seems rooted to the spot. Shakespeare taunts him.

SHAKESPEARE: What? Thought you were tough, Dappo. Thought you could beat me up with one hand tied behind your back.

Dappo steps towards him uncertainly.

SHAKESPEARE: Call yourself a bad man?

DAPPO: Fuck off.

SHAKESPEARE: Want to know who I thought about when I was grinding the mattress, Dappo?

DAPPO: Don't say it.

SHAKESPEARE: I would just imagine your face.

Dappo charges at him, grabs him around the neck, strangling him. Norman struggles to try and separate them. Shakespeare seems almost peaceful and doesn't resist much.

DAPPO: You think I would take it forever? You think you can beat me and force me to suck you and I would let you get away with it?

NORMAN: Dappo, this is Shakespeare. Shakespeare! He wouldn't harm a fly.

DAPPO: I was fourteen then but I am a man now. Try it and see what happens. Fourteen. You thought you would send me away and nobody would ever know? You thought you could tell my mother lies about me and the truth would never come out? You thought I would turn my back on a fight forever?

NORMAN: You've defeated him now, Dappo. You're the winner now. Let him go. Mission accomplished, boy.

DAPPO: At fourteen how was I to fight you off? Fourteen, you cunt. Fourteen years old.

Norman finally manages to get Dappo off Shakespeare. They all collapse, exhausted. Dappo begins to cry in great wracking sobs.

SHAKESPEARE: I'll kill your stepfather for you, if you like.

NORMAN: We all will.

The sobs gradually turn into laughter.

DAPPO: What you going to do, talk him to death, teacher? A schizo, an obsessive compulsive and a lonely nurse. Killer squad.

Suddenly, searchlights are switched on, and the sound of the bulldozers roar into life again. Light sears in through the windows and the open door. They are pinned down by it and have to scuttle into the half shadows.

NORMAN: Time to leave, gentlemen. We can't hide in the dark forever.

SHAKESPEARE: Why don't they come and talk to us? Is that too much to ask?

NORMAN: Is hard to look a man in the eye when you destroying his world, Shakespeare. You all right there, Dappo?

DAPPO: Fine. Healthy. Strong.

NORMAN: Good. I've did my best to prepare you for this.

DAPPO: Maybe the old bitch is dead and I've inherited the house and land in the hills.

He heads to the door. He can barely see beyond the lights. He turns back into the ward

DAPPO: You know how to plant yam, teacher? You ever do any hard work with those hands?

SHAKESPEARE: An educated man can learn.

DAPPO: (*To the voices*) This is my decision, not yours. I'm not listening to you. I said I'm not listening to you. Shut up!

SHAKESPEARE: He'll never make it on his own out there, you realize that. I have to go with him. We'll be all right. I know my way in the world.

NORMAN: Unless he has his medication, he will only get worse, Shakespeare.

SHAKESPEARE: What else would you have me do?

NORMAN: I don't know. I don't know anything anymore. I'm sorry. I tried to fight for you all but I didn't know the rules. Forgive me.

SHAKESPEARE: He will need someone around to guide him.

DAPPO: Where you think you going? I look like I need company to you?

Dappo strides towards the door and into the night. Shakespeare trots after him, then pops back in to pick up his slippers. At the door he turns again.

SHAKESPEARE: Sorry. Forgetting my manners. Too much excitement. It was nice knowing you. Thank you for everything you've done for us.

NORMAN: It wasn't much.

SHAKESPEARE: More than you know.

NORMAN: You're very welcome.

DAPPO: (*From offstage*) If you coming, come. I don't have all night.

SHAKESPEARE: You going to be all right?

NORMAN: Fine. Right as rain.

Shakespeare departs. Norman tidies his desk and then the rest of the ward, then goes to the door. The bulldozers approach, rumbling and roaring. The flashing orange light gets brighter and brighter. Instead of going through the door, he locks himself inside the ward and climbs to where Gonzales usually perched. He takes the pebbles from his pocket and turns them over slowly in his hands. He is alone as the bulldozers close in and bring the walls of Ward 11 crashing down.

THE END

Patricia Cumper began writing for the theatre in the Caribbean in her early twenties. She wrote and had produced over a dozen plays, many of which won awards or writing competitions. They include *The Rapist* which was published in a collection called *Champions of the Gayelle* and *The Fallen Angel and the Devil's Concubine* which has been produced throughout the Caribbean, in the US and Canada. A recent production of *Fallen Angel* in Toronto won two industry awards.

Reviews of her contribution to Black theatre are included in publications by Oxford University Press, Heinemann and Collins.

Since arriving in the UK twenty years ago, she has been commissioned by Talawa Theatre Company, Carib Theatre Company, The Royal Court, Blue Mountain Theatre, BBC Radio 4 and the World Service. *The Key Game* was produced by Talawa at the Riverside, won four-star reviews and was included in *Time Out*'s critic's choice.

She has done a great deal of drama work in radio, including *Westway*, a BBC World Service drama serial. Her five-part radio drama series *One Bright Child* won the CRE radio drama award. Adaptations for radio include Rita Dove's *Darkest Face of the Earth*, Andrea Levy's *Small Island*, Alice Walker's *Color Purple* (which won a silver Sony Award) and Zora Neil Hurston's *Their Eyes Were Watching God*. Commissioned work included a series *The Immigrants* for Radio Berkshire, two short stories and a five part drama for the *Writing The Century* radio drama series.

She worked as Assistant Director on *Blest Be The Tie* at the Royal Court and on *Ska Ba Day* at Greenwich Theatre and recently directed *Jab Molassie*, a carnival adaptation of Stravinsky's *The Soldier's Tale*. She is currently writing and directing a solo actor performance *The Ballad of John Simmonds* at the National Maritime Museum about a sailor who fought at Waterloo.

From February 2006 to March 2012, she was Artistic Director and Chief Executive Officer of Talawa Theatre Company, the UK's foremost Black theatre company. She is currently a board member of English Touring Theatre, Spare Tyre Theatre Company and Standing of the Shoulders of Giants Theatre Company.

OTHER BOOKS ON CARIBBEAN THEATRE

Olivier Stephenson
Visions and Voices: Conversations with Fourteen Caribbean Playwrights
ISBN: 9781845231736; pp. 436; pub. November 2013; £19.99

In the 1970s and 1980s Olivier Stephenson was very actively engaged in Caribbean theatre in New York. There he met a number of Caribbean playwrights, either already living there or making visits. He was looking for plays, they for theatres and performers. Out of this connection came this hugely important and unrepeatable collection of fourteen interviews with most of the founding figures of contemporary Anglophone Caribbean theatre. As the preface by Kwame Dawes indicates, the period of the interviews, from the mid 1970s into the 1980s, was a crucial one for the Caribbean theatre, as its most productive and revolutionary period, and a time when it was already taking on the variety of forms and locations that still characterise it today.

Besides talking about their own influences, experiences, goals and aesthetic visions, each playwright contributes to a collective picture of Caribbean theatre being defined by its spaces – diasporic or regional, proscenium or open air; the nature of its audiences – a heated debate about the possibilities for a commercial theatre that has the work of Trevor Rhone at its heart – and the playwright's relationship to inherited theatre traditions and to specifically Caribbean cultural resources. Reflective, analytical, visionary, opinionated – these are lively interviews, not least because Olivier Stephenson asked each of the playwrights for their views on their peers – views sometimes given with acerbic frankness.

This collection should, of course, have been published many years ago, and the subsequent deaths of eight of the interviewees make it something of a memorial, but the interviews themselves read as freshly as when they were recorded. With extensive annotations and end notes, and insightful introductions by Kwame Dawes and Olivier Stephenson, this is an essential book for anyone interested in contemporary Caribbean theatre and its history.

All our titles can be bought on-line at www.peepaltreepress.com